Women, Writing, and Soul-Making

Creativity and the
Sacred Feminine

Women, Writing, and Soul-Making

Creativity and the Sacred Feminine

PEGGY TABOR MILLIN

 STORYWATER PRESS

Asheville, North Carolina

Published by Story Water Press, PO Box 9803, Asheville, NC 28815
Printed in the United States of America
Copyright © 2009 by Peggy Tabor Millin

COPYRIGHT ACKNOWLEDGMENTS

Cover art, **"Dark Goddess, White Virgin," by Bonnie Temple Cassara** © **2004 Paul Cassara**, used with permission of Paul Cassara.

"Story Water" by Jelaluddin Rumi from *The Essential Rumi,* **trans. Coleman Bark with John Moyne, A.J. Arberry, and Reynold Nicholson** © **1995 Coleman Barks**, with permission of Coleman Barks, Maypop Books, Athens, GA.

Material excerpted from *The Millionth Circle* **by Jean Shinoda Bolen, M.D.** © **1999 Jean Shinoda Bolen M.D.** used with permission of RedWheel/Weiser LLV Newburyport MA and San Francisco, CA www.redwheelweiser.com

Material excerpted from *Pilgrim at Tinker Creek* **by Annie Dillard** © **1974 by Annie Dillard**, reprinted by permission of HarperCollins Publishers.

Material excerpted from **"Wisdom in the Dark Emotions" by Miriam Greenspan, published in** *Shambhala Sun.* **January, 1993,** © **1993 by Miriam Greenspan**, used with permission of Miriam Greenspan, author of *Healing through the Dark Emotions: The Wisdom of Grief, Fear, and Despair.* Boston: Shambhala, 2003.

Material excerpted from *Nine Gates: Entering the Mind of Poetry* **by Jane Hirschfield** © **1997 by Jane Hirschfield**, reprinted by permission of HarperCollins Publishers.

Definitions in this book are from *Merriam-Webster's Collegiate Dictionary. Eleventh Edition.* Merriam-Webster, Inc., Springfield, Mass, 2003.
Personal stories in this book have been altered to honor the privacy of those involved.

ISBN: 978-0-9823711-0-7
Library of Congress Control Number: 2009901299

Book cover and interior design and production by Jane Perini,
Thunder Mountain Design & Communications, www.thundermountaindesign.com
Author photograph (back cover) by Max Poppers, www.silverspiritsphotography.com
Author photograph (inside) by Tracey Schmidt, www.traceyschmidt.com
Graphics by Ginger Graziano, www.gingergraziano.com

Dedication

Susan Trout

Carolyn Wallace

Maggie Wynne

Soul-Filled Friendship
Belief • Trust • Faith • Compassion
Attention • Love • Listening • Support
Creativity • Selflessness • Guidance
Questioning • Challenge • Intelligence
Laughter • Honesty • Tolerance
Gratitude
and so much more

Valerie Leff

For my husband Lou, the yang to my yin,

the ballast to my boat,

my friend, teacher, and love.

In memory of my dear friend and dream partner,

Bonnie Temple Cassara. Her painting "Dark Goddess,

White Virgin" graces the book's cover.

Acknowledgments

With gratitude to all those who have believed,
supported, and assisted:

All present and past class and retreat participants who have illuminated and continue to illuminate the process and its rewards

Kathy Goodwin, who by taking care of business in a forthright and cheerful manner, eases my writing life

Kelle Olwyler, who provides a steady and loving presence and helps me structure my plans and ground the goals I envision

Wayne Caskey, coach and friend, who led me to the wall I had built and waited patiently until it dissolved

Betsy Fletcher, Jeanette Reid, and Maggie and Bob Wynne for writing space in their beach and mountainside homes

Heloise Jones, Virginia McCullough, Martha Jane Petersen, and Anne Scott, who joined other sisters-in-spirit mentioned here in reading and encouraging

Martha McMullen, Madge Murray, and Joan Weiner, who by their continued encouragement, kept me going in the difficult early days

Doris Betts, Cathy Smith Bowers, Tommy Hays, and Peggy Parris, my writing teachers

Tami Ball, Alice Johnson, Wendy Kirkland, Virginia McCullough, and Rachelle Rogers, the critique group who reviewed the early versions

Table of Contents

If I do not do it now,
when else can I do it?

— Dogen Zenji

Introduction

Maybe this is the chance to live and speak the things
I really do believe, that power comes from moving into
whatever I fear most that cannot be avoided.

— Audre Lorde

Writing—a hall of mirrors,
myriad reflections of myself
holding blank pages.
No exit, no partner but fear—
until I listen:
the quiet hum of my heart
the beckoning whisper of my soul—
an invitation to attend,
RSVP engraved in script
and in my hand
a golden pen.

I accept and lose myself
in the dance.

i. The Invitation

The best invitation comes not on gilt-edged vellum, but on the lips of a trusted friend excited to share something precious to her. Within the covers of this book, I would like to be such a friend by sharing with you my journey into writing and my subsequent passion for supporting women in giving voice to their soul's truth.

I want to share the precious and deeply held belief that motivated me to write this book: writing is a means for us, as women, to find our voice and, while on that journey, to reveal our soul. The writing process gently and inexorably strips us clean when we open ourselves to this exploration. Releasing our truth is worth the risk because, when we give voice to our deeper truth, we effect change across seemingly impenetrable barriers. We change the world one word at a time.

ii. For the Reader

Women, Writing, and Soul-Making is an invitation for you to explore the feminine, with all its strengths and vulnerabilities, as the way to claim your creative power, your writing, and your life. You will be shown a process for your writing practice and told why such a practice is helpful and necessary. You will find support and encouragement for your creative journey, which ultimately is the journey to revealing your center, your true self, your soul.

What you will find throughout these pages are insights rather than arguments, suggestions rather than methods, possibilities rather than absolutes. As a result, the content creates space for you, trusting you to interact with what is being said and to create your own path. I invite you to be with the material and to mine it for the answers to the deeper questions it may arouse.

iii. Exploring the Title

I did not give the book its current title until the manuscript was complete. As the title revealed itself, first as a concept and then in words, I felt shifts of energy deep in my belly. I experienced the book as mine in a way I had not done before. *Women, Writing, and Soul-*

Making: Creativity and the Sacred Feminine invites you to explore your writing as your hall of mirrors and to find there the nurturance that will sustain you through all your creative endeavors.

"Women"

Women are psychically, as well as anatomically, different from men. The qualities for which women have long been criticized—empathy, emotional sensitivity, and intuition—are the same qualities that enrich and deepen our writing. In our quest for equal opportunity, I question whether both women and men have lost the gift of difference.

While attending and teaching mixed gender classes, I noticed the ways in which we women either gave our power to the men or had to fight to earn our say. Those of us who had no difficulty being open and honest in women's groups held back when even one man was present. We restricted our writing so that it revealed, not our truth, but our accommodation to male-prescribed norms. Fear of belittlement and rejection, of being misunderstood or unheard—all these fears and more—restrained us from discovering and speaking our truth.

Finding ourselves as writers, especially if we have somehow lost ourselves in our lives, requires focus on process, not product. When focused on process, we become inner directed. For the feminine, the creative urge is internal and demands

Writing provides the way for us to discover how to synthesize feminine being with masculine doing. By taking a feminine approach to writing and embodying it consciously, we more easily integrate creative process with written product.

playfulness, a letting go of limitations, and an opening to possibility. From this place, our intuition leads us toward a productive outcome.

"Writing"

I view writing as a path for women to claim their inner power as writers and as women. Writing provides the way for us to discover how to synthesize feminine *being* with masculine *doing*. By taking a feminine approach to writing and embodying it consciously, we more easily integrate creative process with written product. This exploration frees us to be wholly ourselves.

We only need to be willing to learn who we are and what the depth of our soul truly wants and needs to express. While sharing our writing in a safe circle, we learn to trust this process and thereby trust ourselves.

When we focus on producing a product by listening to an outer call, we are likely to become attached to the outcome in terms of success as measured by money and fame. We lose our center with this approach and easily collapse into old patterns of defining ourselves by pleasing others.

Focus on outcome has given rise to a whole genre of "how-to-write" books that offer everything from how to write a mystery to how to make a million dollars with our own "how-to-write" book. To reduce writing to steps toward a goal deprives authors, readers, and the work itself of the inspirational function of art. The day of the "how-to" is over. No one can tell us "how to" about anything but the most concrete assembly—anyone who has tried assembling a bicycle from instructions knows that even then it is intuition and experience that make it finally come together as a functional whole.

With sustenance from a supportive writing community of our own gender, the writing does the work. We can overcome the individual and cultural messages impacting our self-identity. We need never address those messages directly. Instead, the writing of random memories and experiences, fictional or fact, clarifies thought and over time reveals patterns and themes. We do not need to analyze ourselves or dredge up memories or work on self-improvement. We only need to be willing to learn who we are and what the depth of our soul truly wants and needs to express. While sharing our writing in a safe circle, we learn to trust this process and thereby trust ourselves.

"Soul-Making"

I use the term *soul-making* as it was used by the nineteenth-century English poet John Keats. He believed that the soul was distinct from rational intelligence, but was affected by it. In his view, the soul was formed by three influences: 1) rational intelligence, including our educational learning, 2) the heart, including feelings and emotions, and 3) our experience in the school of life. In contrast to a traditional Christian view of life on earth as a "vale of tears," an experience of darkness and suffering from which we escape only through divine redemption, Keats saw the world as a "vale of Soul-making," a classroom providing lessons necessary for the evolution of our souls.

A Cherokee wood carver gave me a metaphor for soul-making when he explained, "The wood reveals to me the image it holds. Then I remove everything except that." Likewise, soul-making is a process of revealing what is already there. As we grow and engage in inner exploration, we discover and peel away old beliefs, erroneous assumptions, and meaningless rules and restrictions imposed by family, society, and culture. Contrary to what we may believe, we are not called to self-improvement in the sense of acquiring some knowledge or skill so we can "get better." We are called to winnow away all that is not the perfected soul we already are. This process allows us to fulfill our destiny and express it in our life's work.

By examining Keats's three influences on the soul, we can conclude that American culture strongly believes in the power of the intellect and rationality while it devalues, and even fears, feelings and emotions. Further, our culture teaches us to interpret experience through the lens of duality as good/bad or right/wrong and does not support using experience to evolve the soul.

Because we are women, we are closely aligned with the soul. We have retained a connection with our emotions and are willing to connect to our inner life. Our intelligence is influenced by and sometimes derived from our emotional life, our bodies, and our intuition. This blend of heart and intellect enables us to more easily perceive commonalities within differences, seek cooperation instead of competition, and find nonviolent approaches to conflict.

"Creativity"

I cannot speak of the creative journey *as* a journey unless I name its obstacles—the primary one being fear. Fear and its cousin doubt can wreak havoc in every woman's creative life, no matter how outwardly successful she becomes. All creativity requires both courage and fearlessness. Courage is defined in *Merriam-Webster's 11th Collegiate Dictionary* as "mental or moral strength to venture, persevere, and withstand danger, fear, or difficulty." I interpret this to mean that when faced with a challenge, we garner the strength to embrace it.

Courage implies an impetus to action, a response to outer threats and obstacles. Fearlessness applies courage to the task of exploring our inner selves; by practicing fearlessness, we learn not to fear what lies within us.

Fearlessness is an invitation to experience the world just as it is and just as we are.

Think about this: as a writer, you have faced self-doubt at some time. You hear voices that say, "I can't," "I don't know how," "I'll never be good enough," and so on. Yet, almost as soon as you hear these voices, *when you listen*, you hear a quieter voice that counters, "Even so, I must find a way," "I can learn," "I *will* write." I believe that voice comes from the soul, our deepest truth—whatever name you want to give that soft-spot-within that may tremble and hide, but never gives up. To awaken our soft spot requires exposing our vulnerabilities.

To be writers, we must be in touch with our soft spot or we cannot create believable worlds and characters who are fully human. Chogyam Trungpa Rinpoche, a Buddhist teacher, taught that fearlessness arises from tenderness—we open our hearts to the world knowing the tenderness that is there. In this view, fearlessness is an invitation to experience the world just as it is and just as we are.

As fearless writers, we accept the challenge of being alive and fully and wholly human. We learn to love ourselves as our first obligation to word and to world. We cannot write or serve without embracing who we are—all of it—without judgment.

"The Sacred Feminine"

I encountered Mary, Queen of Peace, on a pilgrimage to Medjugorje, Yugoslavia—now Bosnia—in 1989. The sparse knowledge I had of Marian apparitions was gleaned shortly before the pilgrimage. Raised a Protestant and a student of Eastern spiritual practices, I had little experience of a feminine divinity or of Mary as mother of Jesus. I was astonished to learn that Pope John Paul I had said, "God is Father, but above all, God is Mother." As a result of my experience on the pilgrimage, I developed a personal relationship with Mary, whose presence in my life expanded over time into a guiding feminine energy.

Lord Mother is whom we have been missing, and she is the one we have been searching for. She will manifest within us and through us. We are her body and her voice, her spirit and her soul in all its crazy-quilt diversity. Her arrival is up to us, the women of the earth.

This sacred feminine energy, which I later named "Lord Mother," emanates the nurturing, sustaining, comforting, and generative energy of the Universe. Lord Mother is the progenitor, the Mother of All Life, the earth. She calls women to give voice to their soul's truth through their talents, strengths, and destinies.

We return to the sacred feminine to reconnect with something we know within but have temporarily forgotten. We may have no template for a feminine face of God. We may be confused by the very thought of the possibility. I cannot provide a definition. I believe that the sacred defined is the sacred limited. I can only say I experience it as a deep sense of expansive energy in my heart. You must discover for yourself what the sacred feminine holds for you. Lord Mother is whom we have been missing, and she is the one we have been searching for. She will manifest within us and through us. We are her body and her voice, her spirit and her soul in all its crazy-quilt diversity. Her arrival is up to us, the women of the earth.

iv. The Process before the Product

I had nearly completed a manuscript on women and writing when I knew I had made the mistake of writing for publishers rather than writing from my own understanding. I started over.

When I tried to create a new outline, nothing came. I filled journals with notes, my belly cramped, and the words were not cohesive. Very slowly I understood the message: if I was to reflect the feminine approach to writing that I teach, I had to write the book *from* the feminine. The feminine writes in circles, makes leaps, tells the truth with dream, imagery, and metaphor, and relies on inner knowing. The masculine approach makes outlines, develops linearly from premise to conclusion, and relies on outside authority.

I perused my journals and chose *writes*, spontaneous freewrites I had written to prompts along with my class participants. Freewriting is the technique of writing rapidly by hand without pause to edit or think. Freewriting allows us to outrace the conscious mind. The prompts consist of single words, phrases, pictures, or objects. In this instance, I used freewrites as further prompts to explore women and writing. The resulting writes are presented here at the beginning of each *word circle*—a term I invented to reflect the feminine approach because the word *essay* defines a masculine hypothesis/argument/conclusion format.

After completing a few word circles, I knew I could not write the book without some masculine discernment and order. I had a heart-to-heart talk with the book, begging for a structure. I was guided to take a large sheet of paper and on it draw a circle for each word circle. I wrote in the name of the write and the subjects discussed. I also drew additional circles and penciled in subjects I thought I might discuss in word circles yet to be written. This was my guide—not a line at all, but a series of circles, the order of which I trusted would be revealed. Sometimes I felt I was laboring through mud even though I knew well what I wanted to say. I learned that this "mud" *is* the way the feminine approaches tasks. I revisited each topic, coming closer and closer through an intuitive, as opposed to a cognitive, sorting process.

Once the basic content was in place, the skills of my masculine-based education—analysis, grammar, organization—took control. The book no longer objected to the shaping and manipulation needed to allow readers to enter. In fact, the revision and editing process revealed another level of understanding. Each word circle stood independent of the others while the interconnections between two or more had grown many layered and varied. Concepts deepened with each visit to the material. I had sunk into the darkness of creativity and then brought my creation up into the light. The book developed like a tree reaching for the sun, taking a shape I had never imagined.

v. The Passion behind the Pen

Beyond my resume of academic credentials, published writing, and teaching experience, I am a risk taker who craves safety and security. Whatever I have learned, it has been because something inside of me has pushed me from a comfortable place out onto the edge. In my childhood, I integrated many messages that taught me that speaking out could be risky and that I had no right to my point of view. Countering these messages became my destiny; I would find the means to communicate my truth and support others in doing the same. I now believe

Writing is my soul's expression; writing is how I continue to know myself as a woman and as a writer.

that the journey toward claiming our creative expression is also the journey toward freeing our soul. Writing is my soul's expression; writing is how I continue to know myself as a woman and as a writer.

Throughout my career as a student and professional, I ascribed no value to my writing because it came easily to me. Also, in my mind it was not "real" writing because it was not fiction or poetry, the writing I assumed truly creative people did. I never paid attention to the A's on my papers or the many compliments on letters, or that I was the one to write the grant proposals, publicity releases, and brochure copy. I believed I had nothing of my own to say and that no one would listen to me. In short, I was terrified at the notion of stretching beyond the safe box-sides I had erected for myself.

My confession may be of use to other women who feel this way about their writing. We fear we are the only ones who do not know how, cannot begin, and who judge our words as unworthy. We carry our fear in a brown paper wrapper buried in the bottom of a suitcase packed tight with busy lives: our relationships, the way in which we earn our right to exist (career, parenting, cleaning, entertaining, volunteering), and our distractions (shopping, browsing the Internet, television). If we stop long enough to examine this suitcase, we must choose between exploring the fear and its relation to our lives and closing the lid on curiosity and possibility.

I believe if you have read this far, you are somewhere on your journey into fearlessness. I invite you to use this book as a companion. I trust that you will read slowly and with your heart and belly as well as your mind. Each time you return to the book, you have the opportunity to dive deeper and discover a new level of yourself.

I grew up in Blythe, California. The desert that raised me is flat with no vegetation so stately as the saguaros and no yellow primroses or rocks to break the barren monotony. Even the mountains seem to retreat from the landscape, appearing as distant purple humps escaping over the horizon.

Inside me is an open expanse like the desert on which I was raised. For years I believed this inner space should be filled with facts and figures. I thought it was dead and barren, unable to birth anything worthwhile.

Over time, however, lying in this nothing brownness as I sometimes did on the sand near my desert home, I began to notice how brown serves. How everything that lives arises from the apparent nothingness of brown. How life is not so much represented by green as by the steadfastness of brown— the soil, the tree trunks, the rocks, the river silt. How, while the male birds are often flashy with reds and blues and yellows, the females who birth the eggs are shades of brown.

I saw this landscape inside me, a mirror of the desert itself—a place of camouflage and flickering shadows. The rock shifts and becomes a horned toad, the stick moves and is a lizard, the snake appears from the shadow of crusted earth. The silhouettes of turkey vultures loop down the arroyo, and a cactus wren chuk-chuk-chuks from inside a creosote bush.

I discovered the value hidden in what I thought was the void of my soul and learned to appreciate the wind soughing as it rubbed the grains of sand to make them sing and set the dust devils dancing along the mesa. Somewhere in my childhood I ate the desert, digested it, made it into bone and sinew, learned from it how to breathe, learned about waiting, about the vast spaciousness of the soul, and how subtle the shifts are that take us closer to Home.

Word Circles

Story Water

A story is like water
that you heat for your bath.

It takes messages between the fire
and your skin. It lets them meet,
and it cleans you!

Very few can sit down
in the middle of the fire itself
like a salamander or Abraham.
We need intermediaries.

A feeling of fullness comes,
but usually it takes some bread
to bring it.

Beauty surrounds us,
but usually we need to be walking
in a garden to know it.

The body itself is a screen
to shield and partially reveal
the light that's blazing
inside your presence.

Water, stories, the body,
all the things we do, are mediums
that hide and show what
is hidden.

Study them,
and enjoy this being washed
with a secret we sometimes know,
and then not.

— Jelaluddin Rumi

ONE

Peeling Carrots with Emily Dickinson

The secret of seeing is, then, the pearl of great price.
If I thought he could teach me to find it and keep it forever
I would stagger barefoot across a hundred deserts after any
lunatic at all. But although the pearl may be found, it may not
be sought. The literature of illumination reveals this above all:
although it comes to those who wait for it, it is always, even to
the most practiced and adept, a gift and a total surprise.

— Annie Dillard

his morning I lay in bed wanting to remain dressed in my green sheets,
kissed by the cool spring breeze. I do not like lying in bed, but this
morning changed all that. I felt I could lie there forever. Then what I
saw beyond the window caused me to rise and rush from the bedroom,
passing my husband, saying, "Have you looked outside?" He was reading
the news on the computer, enthralled by the drama of political power plays.
I didn't care. I was on my journey to the deck to see dawn wash pink gold
over the hills and trees to waken the birds.

As easily as I had been captivated by the morning, I cast it aside for rou-
tine. I ran to the moment, but did I savor it? Each gentle stroke of breeze on
my skin, the faint perfume of the flowers, the song of the fountain on rock?

The other night, as I reached for silverware, I remembered to be aware. I
stopped to feel the slick surface of the fork handle and the weight of the knife,
to see my concave reflection in the spoon. I shut the drawer with total presence,
turned, and forgot. I became just me moving through to the next activity.

i. Romancing the Muse

As I write, I become aware of the heel of my right hand pushing
across the mild roughness of the notebook. I attend to the pressure of
my thumb and forefinger pressing the pen against my middle finger.
I wonder at the way my body translates unconscious thoughts into
symbols and script. I listen to the slide-slide rhythm of my hand and
the silence of my breathing.

This moment of awareness—my hand now partially on the rose-

When I drop the question into the silence and leave it alone, an intuitive knowing of the answer usually arises to take me to the next step.

wood table, my thigh pressing the hard edge of the chair, the hum of the refrigerator, a mockingbird singing counterpoint to the wind chime—this moment of awareness allows me to be present to myself. I read that Walt Whitman said this is where a poem comes from: the space produced when a focused activity of the body overtakes the mind.

The mind finds a restful state when the body occupies itself in some repetitive physical activity that requires attention but not thinking. Into this space in our thoughts, Imagination, Intuition, and Inspiration—the Muse Collective—arise like self-seeding plants to offer fruit for the picking. The relationship between physical work and the Muse could explain why Emily Dickinson's poems began as scribbles on slips of paper tucked into her apron pocket as she accomplished household chores. Perhaps if she'd had the leisure to sit all day at her desk, the Muse would have stayed in the kitchen waiting for her to peel the carrots.

May Sarton found her Muse in the garden. Other authors cite walking, showering, and driving as activities that invoke the Muse. When stumped on a project, I take on a household chore that at other times I would call drudgery—cleaning the refrigerator, taking a toothbrush to the tile grout, organizing the pantry, pulling weeds. I've had to explain to friends who have loaned me their house as a writing retreat that I super-cleaned not because the house was dirty, but because I needed the inspiration that so often comes when I do menial work.

A contemplative practice provides a similar opportunity. In meditation, I am engaged and focused on sitting and breathing. Thoughts race through my mind like clouds crowding the sky, but if I notice them and let them go, they space themselves farther and farther apart. My meditation teacher advises students to take a question into meditation. When I drop the question into the silence and leave it alone, an intuitive knowing of the answer usually arises to take me to the next step.

ii. Three Steps, One Dance

First Step: Out of Our Heads, Into Our Bodies

Women trained in academia or who have written as part of their jobs, whether grants, reports, scholarly papers, or marketing materials, often experience particular hardship when making the shift from head to belly, from mental control to physical allowing, from thought to feeling.

A newspaper veteran, Carol wrote interviews and a personal interest column. Meredith was a professional storyteller and award-winning speaker. In response to any prompt, each produced complete and polished anecdotal stories with beginnings, middles, and ends even when given no time frame for the writes. Still, Carol and Meredith both felt detached from their writing and knew it lacked an essential quality they wanted—the visceral and emotional sense of connection between the writer and the story.

For our writing to be more than wonderful words gracefully connected into lyrical prose, more than an anecdote or a good column, we must risk writing *from* the story content and not *about* it. Writing *about* is reporting. Writing *from* requires us to put ourselves into the story—our emotions, feelings, vulnerabilities. Not that we must detail our personal experience, but our willingness to explore our inner feelings in relation to the material creates an emotional container for our words. We become as present to the material as we are to peeling carrots or weeding or cleaning grout.

Being present requires being *centered* in our bodies. To find the center in the body, we sit erect in a relaxed posture that allows the whole body to breathe easily. Our physical center is approximately midway between the naval and the womb space. We breathe deeply, filling the belly and pulling the breath up through the solar plexus, heart, and throat, and releasing in the exhalation. In this way, we soften the belly and release tension throughout the body.

Once we recognize how being centered feels, we can do it at any time in any situation simply by straightening our spine and breathing into our bellies. We lose the centered feeling when we stay in our heads figuring things out, or when we allow our emotions to overwhelm us with angst and drama. Centering unites head, emotion, and body with the earth beneath our feet. The mind relaxes and an inner stillness descends even in the midst of outer chaos.

REMEMBER TO BREATHE. A friend's computer screen floated this message on the screensaver. Breathing does it. A few slow, deep, conscious breaths into the belly are all we need to bring us into ourselves.

Second Step: Freewriting Frees Us

Freewriting is a rapid-writing technique commonly recommended for personal journal writing, for uncluttering the mind before attending to a writing task, and for generating first drafts, exploring possibilities, making character sketches, and so on.

Freewriting allows us to outrace the conscious mind. To freewrite, centered in the vast space of the belly with the critical mind held at bay, we let go to the pen. We give up control and open ourselves to the river of the unconscious. The current may rush us downstream over rapids and across clear pools, or drag us into swirling eddies to sink in unexplored depths. If we try to control this journey, we will be dumped on dry land. When we let go of the idea of getting anywhere and simply follow the pen, writing transitions from being a mental exercise to what naturally occurs when pen meets paper. Freewriting to prompts catches us unaware with the truth, especially, as we shall see, when the prompt is not designed to lead us any particular place.

When we let go of the idea of getting anywhere and simply follow the pen, writing transitions from being a mental exercise to what naturally occurs when pen meets paper.

Just now in typing "freewriting," I wrote "freewiring." A fortuitous mistake. Freewriting does indeed freewire us. Freewriting deconstructs our concretized images of ourselves and forces us to redefine what we think writing is. Once we freewire ourselves, we can truly write free.

Freewriting strips us of the camouflage we wear to hide our fears. Beginning in high school most of us were taught how to avoid being true authors of our work. We learned to attribute ideas to others, with appropriate footnotes. We peppered our own insights or ideas with words like "seems," "appears," "perhaps," or the conditional "one could surmise." The passive voice further assisted us in distancing ourselves from acknowledging our point of view.

Freewriting is best done with time limitations imposed before the write so that we will not be tempted to choose the time based on our preference for the prompt. We set the timer for five to forty minutes. From a bag of words (I cut poems into snippets of single words or short phrases), we blindly choose one and begin to write. Within these limitations, we do not have time to build our equivocations into a sturdy hunter's blind for our own perceptions. No time to don the camouflage. Just write. Concrete experience. Lists of words. Flamboyant. Funny. Nonsensical. Anything goes.

Third Step: Practice Makes Possible

After class, Linda stopped me. "I can see that these writing exercises help me, but where does it go? These other women are wonderful writers, but so what? I think I need to be doing something with it, but I don't know what."

I explained that the practice of writing is the foundation of being a writer. "It isn't a step to something better, it *is* writing. From this, all your work springs. But you have to do it."

"Like scales?" she said.

"Exactly. No matter how good or how great or how accomplished a musician gets, she has to practice her scales. With writing, it helps to practice in a group. The group keeps you honest, both in terms of staying with the practice and in terms of writing your truth. This practice is the ground of writing."

Practice does not make perfect; practice makes possible. Practice—of sport, writing, art-making, meditation, music—has no goal but revelation. Practice discovers, uncovers, reveals, surprises, astonishes, and awes. Practice provides the road through new terrain, tests our resolve, and develops our skill. We take the attitude of the adventurer, not rushing but moving slowly enough to notice details. The unexpected occurs. "Everything is food" is an ancient spiritual teaching that can be applied in writing.

I say, once we show up to write, we are written. The experience does not feel like we are at the goal, enlightened, or written because showing up demands that we abandon expectations.

The Dance

When we combine *physical centeredness in the belly* and *freewriting to neutral prompts* with active *practice, both solitary and in community,* we have the choreography for Centered Writing Practice. I name the process and write it with capitals to emphasize its importance, as well as to differentiate it from other freewriting techniques.

We center in our bellies and put the pen to paper. No crossing out or lingering over perfect phrases or searching for metaphors. Following the pen, we outrace the conscious mind. We allow ideas and words to tumble across the page like somersaulting children, unruly and self-absorbed. We practice only to develop the practice of writing. Whether we later appraise the writing as "good" or discover a single gem to develop into a marketable piece does not matter. We practiced, we wrote. That is enough.

In Centered Writing Practice, as in repetitive work and contemplative practices, we focus on an action of the body in order to clear the mind for something new to enter. Psychoanalyst Carl Jung said that once we are on the path, we are at the goal. Zen master Dogen said once we are on the cushion, we are enlightened. I say, once we show up to write, we are written.

The experience does not feel like we are at the goal, enlightened, or written because showing up demands that we abandon expectations. After long years of meditation practice, I was introduced to Soto Zen, which directs one to "just sit." No instructions follow this directive other than to hold correct posture. There are no breathing techniques or mantras. No meaning is attached to the feelings, emotions, altered states, or visions that may float past like dandelion fluff on a summer breeze. Everything centers on being present in the body in the moment.

Just sit. No striving. No attachment. Stay present on the cushion, centered in the body, grounded. When I followed these directions, my established practice fell apart. I could not focus. I watched my mind fill with thoughts tumbling and jumping and poking at me for attention. Discouraged, I called the teacher for direction. She laughed and told me that if I was aware of this tumult, I had made a big leap forward. "Nothing's wrong," she said. "Now you are aware of what your mind has been doing all along." I then understood that inside the mind of each meditator perched on a black *zafu* in perfect lotus position, eyes on the white wall, there existed a hyperactive and hysterical crowd of thoughts. I was not alone. There was nothing to attain, no place to go. With good reason, meditation teachers use the word *practice*. Greeted with non-judgment, everything that occurs in practice enlightens.

iii. Circling the Wagons

Life is full of metaphors. My naming of Centered Writing Practice coincided with my giving up the cramped downtown office where my participants had to huddle around a table to write. I began leading groups in my home. Here, in the company of family quilts, we sit in a circle unshielded by tables. Vulnerable. Open. Afraid. Excited. Expectant.

The practice that refines and shapes women's writing requires a group, at least periodically. When women feel stress, they are biologically wired to seek solace with other women. The hormone oxytocin interacts with estrogen to trigger a "tend-and-befriend" response. In women, this urge to group for safety is stronger than the "fight-or-flight" response generated by adrenalin. In the face of emotional risk-taking, women prefer to be surrounded by other women. Trust develops in a circle made safe by mutually accepted boundaries. Such an atmosphere invites the sharing of stories—factual and fictional. Over time, with Centered Writing Practice as the focused activity, the group energy supports each woman in finding her voice and exploring her soul's truth.

A group of women writers provides the support needed to deal with the judgmental voices in our heads. We learn we are not alone, that every woman present feels inadequate as well as determined, is sometimes afraid as well as hopeful, and needs the support and validation of others. Without naming it, we become aware that we have an Observer within us who can watch how we do what we do without judging.

The Observer enables us to do two things at once. We can swing at a golf ball while appraising the swing, respond to our teenager while noticing our tone of voice. We can meditate and note the thoughts streaming across the screen of the mind, and we can write and listen to our inner—usually critical—commentary. When we write, the Critic's loud voice judges the writing as good or bad, picks at word usage, corrects sentence structure, and compares us to others in the group. When we notice the Critic and ask *who is noticing*, the *who* is the Observer. The Observer is "The One Who Is Aware."

iv. The One Who Is Aware

When I first became aware of the Observer, it was a gentle voice giving me the opportunity to change my habitual reactions. It whispered in my ear, "Look at how you choose." I discovered I could

I want to change the age-old dictum "Write what you know" to "Write from what you know toward what you do not know." Write toward and through uncomfortable. Writing then becomes how we discover what we think and who, at heart, we are.

invite the Observer to tap me on the shoulder, warning me *before* I acted or reacted. In writing, engaging the Observer enables us to let the Critic's comments float by like logs on a river. In this way we learn to disengage from self-critique and disregard the Critic's incessant chatter. We continue to write no matter what the Critic says.

This approach to practice allows us to become fearless and more adept as writers. Like a difficult relative, the Critic does not go away. No matter how accomplished we become, it will want to have its say. As with a crotchety aunt or uncle, we do not have to listen. We stay alert to its devious ways by consistent practice of using the Observer.

The Observer allows us to pay attention to our bodies while we engage in the physical act of writing. Our bodies alert us to emotional discomfort, and emotional discomfort signals the near-presence of an unarticulated personal truth. When the body signals, we notice the desire to veer away. Instead of following the impulse, we can choose to write toward the discomfort. As fearless writers, we write past uncomfortable toward the truth.

We allow the thoughts we have hidden even from ourselves to flow from the pen, showing us what we do not know that we know. The revelation contained in our writing is not always direct or recognizable. Like dreams, our writing often reveals its lessons slowly over time. I want to change the age-old dictum "Write what you know" to "Write *from* what you know *toward* what you do not know." Write toward and through uncomfortable. Writing then becomes how we discover what we think and who, at heart, we are.

From our store of experience, we imbue our writing with the feelings and emotions that make it individual. The Observer sharpens the observation of daily life that grounds our writing in concrete sensory detail and fresh perceptions. By using the Observer to report on our internal information—our emotions, feelings, intuitions, and their associated physical twinges and quirks—our writing sinks below the surface of action and description to the feelings and emotions that underlie the universality of human experience. This is how we touch our readers.

Characters, narrators, the "I" of a poem do not float around in a vacuum. We create the world in which they exist either by reliving our experience or extrapolating from it. This new world may be one with pepperoni pizza, buses trailing exhaust, and a plastic doll lying in the dry yellow grass by the curb. Notice how each object in this simple list evokes a subtle physical response and holds a different emotional tone. The pizza brings images of friends or lonely nights in front of the TV. The bus with its suffocating fumes reminds us of leaving and being left behind. Of the three images, the doll grabs us hardest, arousing grief, despair, and concern as we picture it forlorn, forgotten, and unclaimed in the grass by the busy street. The more intense the emotion associated with an image, the greater our desire to know more. Where is the child who owned the doll? What has become of her?

To make the right choice of images in our writing requires focused attention on both our inner and outer worlds. The Observer informs us dispassionately of what it sees, providing a wide opening for the Muse Collective to enter. The Observer tells us when the writing flows free and clear and when it is clogged; it alerts us to when we are writing true and when we are resisting the truth. We practice: neither tight nor loose, severe nor lenient, and neither too rigid nor too relaxed. The more we practice, the more we notice, and the more quickly we adjust.

v. Making Friends with Our Writing

When I describe Centered Writing Practice, a listener sometimes responds, "Oh, like journaling."

Writing in community provides support, nurturance, and reinforcement for our creative efforts. A community of writers keeps us honest about our intent to write.

"No," I say, and this is why. When most people say "journaling," they refer to the personal journal writing that focuses on daily concerns—relationships, experiences, and problems. Although I have heard journaling dismissively called "write and cry," personal writing is an effective way to find solutions, solve problems, and heal emotional and physical wounds. Journaling also works to empty out emotional distractions so we can better focus on whatever task is at hand. Unlike journaling, Centered Writing Practice focuses on the writing rather than on the writer. We surrender to the pen and trust it to take us where we need to go.

In *Becoming a Writer*, written in the 1930s, author and creative writing teacher Dorothea Brande urged us to write for half an hour as soon as possible upon waking and before talking or reading. "Write whatever comes into your head," she exhorts, later saying, "…what you are actually doing is training yourself, in the twilight zone between sleep and the full waking state, simply *to write*."

When we reach the amount we can write without strain in our half hour, she asks us to push ourselves to write more until we reach a new plateau. Then, as we wish, we can drop back to some mid-level of time and productivity. Brande's intent for this and subsequent exercises in her book is to train us to write on schedule as well as to write any time and any place. At this point, we can move from stream of consciousness writing, or freewriting, to writing toward a specific form, such as a short story, essay, or poem.

I formulated Centered Writing Practice to provide the bridge between freewriting and form. This bridge consists of two elements: writing to neutral prompts and writing in community. Neutral prompts are concrete nouns, active verbs, phrases, objects, or photographs that have no intended emotional connections. For example, the word "mother" is neutral, whereas "my mother" evokes an emotional connection that will tend to lead the writer toward personal exploration. The neutrality of the prompt opens a free and easy connection between the creative impulse and a form or product. Writing in community provides support, nurturance, and reinforcement for our creative efforts. A community of writers keeps us honest about our intent to write. Group members inspire us to keep writing and model habits and methods we can adopt for ourselves. Mainly, the community keeps us writing.

Centered Writing Practice is how we make friends with our writing. Surrendering to the practice and the process presents us with the opportunity for tapping into the open, unbounded spaciousness of universal awareness. This is not a goal of Centered Writing Practice, and we cannot make it happen. Yet, when it does, we recognize the moment by its flow—that miraculous feeling of being one with the writing, of forgetting ourselves in the process, of releasing time and effort. Once experienced, we will always write toward it, inviting its return. We practice surrender, an essential step in opening to creativity. We let go of the writing and release all goals and evaluative measures. We practice noticing and articulating what we have seen, smelled, heard, tasted, and felt.

I find I use the practice in different ways and at different times. The majority of my freewriting comes in the form of Centered Writing Practice responses written in classes with my students. These writes I keep in dated spiral notebooks. In other notebooks, I use Centered Writing Practice to develop some of these writes into poems, stories, or essays. If a developed write beckons me to make it cohesive, I usually switch to writing on the computer. When I get stuck, I return to the notebook, writing by hand until the writing leads me out.

In small notebooks and on scraps of paper in car and purse, I jot down overheard conversations, ideas that come while driving, details and insights that occur when I'm not at home. These may become prompts for writes or make their way whole into a project. I also keep a journal of my nighttime dreams and my interpretation of them. The latter is my current form of personal journaling, the place where I can ferret out my innermost thoughts and feelings in order to keep growing. Dreams feed my imagination and sometimes become prompts for further writing.

We want to write because we have experienced the joy of creative expression. Using Centered Writing Practice, we discover that themes, characters, and memories show up on the page without conscious effort. The writing evolves into a product as an inevitable consequence of exploring the process. At any place on the path of pursuing our desire, however, rules, restrictions, and critique can trip us up, luring us away from the creative well and into a futile search for the "right" way to write. We can lose touch with the creative impulse that inspired our journey. Grounding ourselves in writing practice brings us back to ourselves. Grounded in the practice, we can use the rules, restrictions, and critique with a sense of our own authority. Still we continue to practice—generating, developing, exploring our writing and ourselves.

By learning to engage the territory freely and without restraint, we develop a sense of ourselves as writers. Then it is time to acquire the techniques and tools for shaping our writing into form and applying them at our own discretion.

vi. Lento Tempo

Centered Writing Practice is not a panacea or a quick fix. We may practice for a long time and feel nothing is happening, or that our writing has not changed. Like the gestation in the womb, change happens in *lento tempo*, slow time. Women crave *lento tempo* and need it to survive. Slow is the timing of fertilization and incubation, of creative process. Creative writing often resists being manipulated to meet deadlines. We may need to wait on dreams or synchronicity to inspire and guide our work. In *lento tempo*, we learn the wisdom of letting things rest—bread dough, marinara sauce, roasted turkey, babies, tulip bulbs, fresh paint, grief, anger, ourselves. Almost every book of advice on writing suggests putting a manuscript away for a while once it feels complete. Then the final edit can be undertaken with a fresh ear and eye. Centered Writing Practice teaches us patience, to do by not doing.

Through focused attention, we engage watchful listening—to our inner voice and to our experience. What we achieve is not a perfect product, but a spinning spiral of synthesis. The movement of this spiral cannot be driven, hurried, or organized. *Lento tempo* is the natural rhythm of creation—of body, earth, and universe. As such, *lento tempo* is the rhythm of creativity we hear by practicing awareness.

I practice presence while cutting the cantaloupe. I savor the sunrise hidden beneath the asperous skin, the sudden liberation of fragrant musk. I scoop the slippery nest out with my hand, searching through the slick filaments to release the large white seeds, each containing the potential to satisfy bellies hungry for life.

TWO

My Friend's Kitchen

A peaceful revolution is going on,
a women's spirituality movement, hidden in plain sight.
Through circles of women, healing women,
might the culture come around?

. . .

When a critical mass—the hundredth monkey,
or the millionth circle—tips the scales,
a new era will be ushered in
and patriarchy will be over.

— Jean Shinoda Bolen

My friend's kitchen mirrors her heart—a passionate accumulation of what matters to her. The table takes up most of the floor space and is stacked with books on spiritual and personal growth, solicitations from the nonprofits she generously supports, and photos of family and friends, framed and unframed. At the center of the kitchen a refrigerator hums, stuffed beyond the needs of her single life. From its abundance, she can always pull a wide array of green, yellow, and red vegetables to slice into a colorful salad or succulent soup that delights her guests with aromatic surprises.

The kitchen melts into the living room along a wall lined floor to ceiling with books awaiting the library ladder she plans to buy one day. Plants thrive near the large glass door through which she watches the birds at the feeder or, in spring, the wrens nesting in the hanging ivy.

Visiting her is like entering a small boat where I am repeatedly moving things from one place to the next to free the right surface for sitting or eating. I never mind. We bend over our turquoise cups of fragrant tea and speak of our dreams, fears, failings, and successes, or we sit in silence with the honey of sweet acceptance on our tongues.

i. The Hearth

The hearth was once a circle in the middle of the floor containing the fire that was tended by the woman of the house. She carried a live coal from her mother's hearth to her own at marriage. One of her most important duties lay in keeping the coals alive. Around the hearth, at one home or another, women gathered to share information and gossip while they did handwork—mending, carding wool, knitting, and sewing. In warm weather, they gathered outside on porches and in barns to winnow wheat, shell beans, and shuck corn. They also gathered to assist in birth, illness, and death.

In the summer of 1965, I was a guest in a rural Greek home. The men had taken the sheep to the greener pastures of the mountains while the women and children remained behind. One morning I followed the sound of singing to the barn where women sat on the floor or low stools stringing and sorting tobacco. The golden light of dawn permeated the hard-packed dirt of the yard, the fieldstone walls of the barn, and the leathered faces and hands of the women. An ancient song in minor key echoed off the rafters and drifted across the heads of the brown chickens pecking their way among the grasses along the whitewashed courtyard walls.

It is true that the loss of the hearth is linked to a change in the roles of women, and it follows that women can also provide a hearth from which the new model will evolve.

In my own childhood, women gathered in kitchens at the church fellowship hall for wedding receptions, midweek suppers, and sing-a-longs, at the Farm Bureau square dances, and in my family's home at holiday dinners. When I was twelve, I hovered in the kitchen doorway to be given jobs setting tables or tending smaller children. Inside the kitchen, the women talked as they worked, lowering their voices on tender subjects, laughing, and sometimes crying in the arms of one or more friends.

As I grew older, I was allowed into the kitchen and into the secret world of women, although some conversations remained whispered, or women stopped talking when they saw me. While I am grateful for men's willingness to wash dishes and cook, a circle of women in a kitchen remains sacred to me. In those moments, I am conscious of the live coal within me, tended by generations of women, and mine to pass along.

Circling the Center

One dictionary definition of *hearth* is "a vital or creative center," traditionally identified with the kitchen. The twenty-first century, however, finds fewer families cooking and eating together—in fact, it finds fewer families in the traditional sense. We can lament the loss of the physical hearth and all it represents, casting around for whom to blame, or we can focus on what new vital center might rise in its stead. It is true that the loss of the hearth is linked to a change in the roles of women, and it follows that women can also provide a hearth from which the new model will evolve.

On her compact disc recording, *A Prasad for Women,* Debra Roberts tells of being in a group in Santa Fe when Thomas Banyacya, a Hopi elder, came to speak. He had been asked by his elders to share some ancient predictions. He explained that traditionally women had been in charge of the table that nurtured the family; now, he said, it was time for women to take charge of the table that is the earth. One by one, he bent close to each woman in the group and asked, "Will *you?*"

More recently, in his book *God Has a Dream,* Bishop Tutu wrote that women, given the courage, have the potential to transform our institutions and make them more humane and more just. "Unleashing the power of women," he says, "has the potential to transform our world in extraordinary and many as yet unimagined ways." He shared this opinion on *The Oprah Winfrey Show* and then leaned toward his famous hostess and said, "Will you do it? Will you?"

A feminine approach always works from the inside out. The new hearth is emerging as individual women around the globe respond to an inner quickening with the courage and commitment to join their voices into a collective One. We are defining the new hearth by discovering together what it truly means to embody our femininity and to speak the truth of that experience. We are forming circles in which to listen, speak our truth, lead, and follow. In the safety of circles, we learn to respect silence, create safety, build trust, set boundaries, resolve conflict, and laugh—at ourselves and at the vagaries of life. Circles include and have no hierarchy. They allow us to see one another face-to-face. Circles of women support, uplift, encourage, protect, and inspire. They also share, instruct, and guide through example. Through circles, we find the courage to fulfill our potential to teach peace and justice. Through circles, we can hold sway over the table of the earth without "waging a war on poverty" or "fighting for peace."

We express the new hearth in individual and creative ways—through writing, artwork, teaching, gardening, and daily interactions. It is not a boardroom or another social justice advocacy group, at least not in the forms to which we are accustomed. New models for leadership and organizations that synthesize feminine with masculine principles are already being taught at places like the Institute for the Advancement of Service in Alexandria, Virginia.

The Millionth Circle

Around the world, women's circles proliferate, many inspired by Jean Shinoda Bolen's book, *The Millionth Circle*, and her website, www.millionthcircle.org. Bolen believes that "circles with a center"— meaning, a spiritual center—generate more circles and that at a certain point these women's circles will shift the consciousness of the world. She refers to the work of biologist Rupert Sheldrake, who postulates that a behavior adopted by a small group extends until it reaches an exact point at which it becomes the habit of the entire group. This phenomena has been demonstrated with monkeys: one monkey discovers how to use a branch as a tool to dig for grubs, and in time the whole troop imitates her. More amazing, however, is that soon the same tool use is noted among monkeys on nearby islands that have no physical contact with the inventor or her troop.

When a circle is centered, its purpose is clear, and the energy of the circle radiates out to attract members who will be most served by it.

ii. Gathering the Unlike-Minded

A community of writers requires diversity rather than like-mindedness. After all, writing is about exploring diverse opinions and points of view. Writing and certain values generally held by women—desire for community, willingness to nurture, pleasure in one another's company, openness of emotional expression—form the metaphorical hearth around which the writing community gathers.

I believe this "hearth" to be sacred and to be present in circles of women who gather for a common purpose. Because the purpose in writing groups *is* writing, defining the sacred nature of the circle too specifically by aligning with any specific spiritual practice can discourage diversity among participants. The formation of a circle of women automatically includes the sacred if the leader invites this energy and holds the space for it. Even a short silence within which members focus on the breath will center the group. When a circle is centered, its purpose is clear, and the energy of the circle radiates out to attract members who will be most served by it. The result is a circle of women with diverse personalities, backgrounds, spiritual practices, and belief systems who are able to unite for the purpose of writing and the sharing of stories.

Although I practice Zen meditation and speak of the benefits of meditation practice frequently in this book, I believe that many paths lead to similar results. Walking, communing with nature, contemplation, and prayer all lead us to the still point in which we meet ourselves and our Source, however we define that.

Identities

My circles have included several women whose sizeable families of origin lived in three-room city apartments. I have heard the stories of those who lived in London, Berlin, and New Jersey during World War II, as well as those raised in rural Tennessee in the twenties and on Fifth Avenue in the eighties. I have had African Americans and Afrikaners; Catholics, agnostics, Baptists, and Jews; a New Age psychic; an Air Force colonel; Methodist, Presbyterian, and Episcopal ministers; those with PhDs and some with GEDs. I learned these identities only by what the women revealed in their writing.

Within the circle, we do not socialize, chat, or ask questions about content. We learn about one another only through what each woman reads from her page.

We derive enormous benefit from

entering a group without these or other identities in tow. We look around the circle and learn names, where people live, why they have come, and nothing more. We do not know who has published, who is a beginner, who has children, or who has a PhD. We know only that the purpose of our presence is to write, whatever our background or motivation. All labels and points of view meet peaceably when we stay on purpose; within the circle, we do not socialize, chat, or ask questions about content. We learn about one another only through what each woman reads from her page. Even then, we cannot be sure if it is fiction or nonfiction, and we agree at the outset not to ask.

Diversity in the group adds energy to our writing. We learn about worlds we have not experienced by listening to others' stories. The courage and struggles of these women feed our souls. We are inspired by rich imagery and word choices and the rhythm and cadence that varies from writer to writer. Everything that comes into the circle nurtures everyone present.

Spiraling Down

Women tend to explore meaning in a circular pattern—meaning that their writing and talking begins on one level and spirals inward to what really matters. Many factors determine whether and where the spiral begins and how deep it goes: time, mood, prompt, and safety are some of the variables. This explains why regular writing practice in a group is particularly important. We have the opportunity to try different things, to get comfortable with risk, to be encouraged in our efforts even when the results sound flat and empty or even nonsensical.

We are so hard on ourselves. Writing practice circles allow us to watch how we self-flagellate, even self-mutilate. We sit in the circle and look at each woman as someone acting out a part of us, speaking our thoughts in a different voice. We hear how tentative this one is, how shy another, how funny and kind and guilty and hurt. We see how hard it is for *her* to claim the quality of her writing.

If we do not tell our story, no one else can tell it, and the story will be lost.

We watch ourselves as envy, judgment, comparison, and admiration arise. If we are fortunate enough to be in a diverse circle of women, we see ourselves older and younger, as immigrants, as rich and not so rich, more educated or less so. The stories shared allow us to look past stereotypes and personas, even past annoyances and personal habits. Diversity of personalities and backgrounds and ages enriches a writing circle and challenges us to learn—and accept—the human experience in all its forms. This, in turn, enriches *our* writing.

Over time we feel our hearts open not only to the other women, but to the parts of ourselves they show us. We begin to claim our disclaimers so we can release the self-deprecations we have held onto so tightly. We quit apologizing for our writing. It is what it is—perhaps not as poetic or imaginative as some, but our story and in our voice. If we do not tell our story, no one else can tell it, and the story will be lost.

iii. Skydiving

A writing practice circle supports us in taking personal risks and speaking truth through the written word. When we write in a centered circle, healing happens. Even though many participants comment, "This is better than therapy," the writing circle is not a therapy group. Although it provides support for taking risks with writing, it is also not

an emotional support group. In fact, if the leader allows the participants to venture into either therapy or emotional support, the circle
will lose its feeling of safety because the purpose of the group and its
egalitarian nature will be lost.

When we give advice or probe into someone's motives or past, we
create an us/them relationship in which one person appears to have
more while the other has less. This is the kind of relationship we are
accustomed to within the Power Principle's hierarchical culture. (*Power
Principle* is a term Jungian analyst Marion Woodman uses to replace
the word *patriarchy*, which is misunderstood as synonymous with the
masculine.) The dark or shadow side of the nurturing nature of wom-
en's impulses to help one another manifests whenever we see someone
as a victim, as temporarily needing something we have while she does
not. We can slip into co-dependencies, creating barriers to honesty. In
a writing practice circle, we honor the process of expressing our wholeness as writers and individuals by trusting each person to take responsibility for herself. If someone needs advice or support, she is responsible
for asking for it outside the circle.

Four Opportunities to Leap

Writing digs deep into our psyches, often surprising us with memories and realizations. As a group, we write to a prompt and then, by
turn, read our piece aloud. The listeners provide positive feedback to
which the reader listens without response.

I have identified four instances during this process that offer trans-
formative opportunities:

While we write, we can be aware we are spiraling down into unspoken truths. Commonly we are not aware of what we write as we are
writing it. The pen moves too fast and our assessing mind is disengaged.

When we read, we hear what we have written and recognize its truth. The very act of reading aloud can feel like falling into a deep pit. Emotion may temporarily strangle us, threatening our ability to speak. The circle waits and listens in silence, holding open the gate for expression while trusting the individual to take care of her own needs.

When we look around the circle and understand that we have been heard, our hearts open. We have given a gift and it has been received. This giving and receiving cycle creates an energetic infinity loop nourishing every person in the group.

When we listen to others respond positively to our writing, we hear how our writing touches others, and we see our experience in a new way. The value of positive feedback should not be underrated. We are so accustomed to giving and receiving correction, suggestion, and criticism that we may feel we cannot learn from hearing what works in our writing. When I give positive feedback, it is common for a woman to disown the compliment by changing the subject or making a joke. As children, many of us learned not to trust compliments and to deflect praise. Specific praise, however, offers encouragement and illuminates a foundation to build on.

Negative feedback disempowers us, discouraging the development of our inner authority as writers. Honest, positive reflection on our work enables us to identify the unique qualities of our writing and illuminates new perspectives on our lives.

Over time we drop self-deprecations, feelings of inadequacy, and fears about our writing into the big swirling heart of the circle, which accepts them all. Then we can plow ahead to take risks we never thought possible.

Undoubtedly, this is one reason that writing and writing circles help us heal. Others hear our words through the screen of their own experience, values, and perceptions. Their comments, while focused positively on the writing, often reveal to us what we have shown but have not been able to see.

Through group practice, the importance of our story is brought home to us, along with the recognition that we are not alone. Over time we drop self-deprecations, feelings of inadequacy, and fears about our writing into the big swirling heart of the circle, which accepts them all. Then we can plow ahead to take risks we never thought possible.

Leadership, A Parachute

A leader is necessary to keep the group focused on writing and by doing so to ensure the safety of the group. The leader's ability to embody her leadership role is as important as her skill in presenting prompts or responding to a member's writing. The leader watches for anything that threatens the safety of the circle, such as a participant who criticizes or one who is perpetually late. She keeps the group on purpose by being prepared, curtailing discussion, and enforcing agreements and boundaries. The leader models what it means to honor both the writing process and the group process by staying aware, listening, and addressing problems when they occur. The circle must be able to depend on the leader to handle any threats to its wellbeing as a group and to give members honest feedback on their progress as writers.

A common misconception among women is that to be egalitarian, groups do not need leaders. Without leadership, groups lose their purpose and with that, the feeling of safety. When a women's group loses purpose, its members tend toward socializing and emotional support. Many women complain that informal writing groups they have attended slowly drifted into social gatherings. While we may enjoy socializing, we will resent the waste of writing time. Even though unspoken, blame and judgment generate competition and lack of trust. What began as a group with a shared interest and purpose disintegrates into one with bad feelings and broken relationships.

A strong leader is one whose ego does not need feeding by the group. Her hallmark is her willingness to be as vulnerable as the group's members by writing and reading with them. She is mature enough to admit her own frailties while correcting the problems those frailties may generate. She leads with both heart and head.

Boundaries, A Safety Net

Taking risks and telling the truth does not give carte blanche for behaviors that threaten the safety of the group. A writing practice circle needs rules as well as a leader; together these are the guardians of group safety. The truth we seek is the soul's truth about our understanding of our experience. This truth paints the stark realities of our past and present in rich color and detail. A writing circle is not the place to proselytize, even about the most worthy of subjects. It is not the place to launch into editorial-type expositions expressing opinions on controversial topics. Our points of view arise from our experience, and if we write from our center, we will communicate them without pontificating.

In 2002, on the first anniversary of the terrorist attack on the World Trade Center, I asked a class to respond to the essay "Leap" by Brian Doyle. I wanted the women to connect to Doyle's immediate, emotional, and very personal writing. I specifically asked them not to engage in political rant or commentary. One woman wrote that she was unsure if she could separate personal from political because she no longer felt safe in her own country. She is Jewish with a son adopted from Central America. Since the attack, she had felt her family could be targeted by the swell of patriotism. Her writing came from a great well of ethnic and maternal emotion. We became part of her experience through the sharing of her writing. As a result, without her telling us, we understood the responsibility of each citizen for the direction of the country. We saw vividly where national fear could lead if we did not pay attention, how quickly it could impact an individual life. We understood that no matter our political stance, her experience was valid for her, and this aroused empathy and expanded our awareness in a far deeper way than if she had lectured us on the evils of nationalism or railed against the government.

The Safety of Numbers

When Kate came into the writing circle at a retreat, she announced she was going to "run toward the lion." In response to our blank looks, she shared an African teaching tale that had inspired her: *Lionesses hunt as a team, forming a semi-circle around the herd of antelope. The male lion, himself a poor hunter, stands at the open side of the circle and roars. If the antelope ran toward the lion's roar, they could escape to safety. Instead, they run away from what seems to be the source of their fear and into the claws and jaws of the lionesses.*

Kate had come with the specific intent to break through a long-held fear that inhibited her writing. Her determination had built up over time, germinated by a comment I had made several years prior when she attended a weekly class. After listening to Kate's repeated disparaging remarks about her "redneck" heritage and what she saw as the cultural aridity of her family, I told her that as a writer, her family and roots, far from being a liability, were her greatest treasure. At the retreat, she shared that my words had made her aware of a specific belief she held about herself and her abilities. The long-held belief had become concretized as fear.

The circle created a safe place in which Kate could do whatever she had to do to make the valiant leap toward her fear. As a group, our job was to trust that she knew what she needed and that the writing would take her there. Our role was to witness her process and to trust our own.

When Kate read her story aloud, we could all see the magic the writing had worked. Her posture, her face, her energy were alight. The story was not yet fully formed nor did the group need it to be. All we needed to do was to respond honestly and with compassion to what she had written and the courage it took to write it. We all knew Kate had crossed a barrier she understood. The writing would take care of itself.

In a writing circle, members notice when someone avoids moving toward a fear. Usually the writer is neither conscious she is emotionally blocking nor that her writing reveals both the problem and the answer. In a situation in which we were giving feedback on one another's manuscripts, two of the women had similar difficulty creating real and believable characters. Patti was unable to see and portray the positive side of characters modeled on her parents, and Marsha was unwilling to explore the dark emotions of her characters.

Intuitively, the other women in the circle responded gently, making suggestions but not confronting. As they nudged each woman toward her fear, I was reminded of watching dogs herd sheep. Over the course of the class, group members nudged Patti and Marsha in the right direction until a deeper understanding was opened by a dream or writing exercise. In Patti's case, she had to find some level of forgiveness for her parents in order to portray them as real people rather than as caricatures. Marsha needed to acknowledge and accept her own faults and frailties in order to portray her characters honestly. The resulting shifts in the quality of these women's work astounded us all.

The circle intuits what to do: when to hold and when to let go. From observing what others in the group need, we learn lessons to apply to our own writing and ourselves.

iv. Writing Our Lives

What we learn in a writing practice circle spills into all parts of our lives. Again and again, I hear women say the circle saved their lives. I believe a writing practice circle strengthens our ability to live with paradox. Our lives are "saved" because we become risk takers without loss of security, responsible without burden, self-reflective without guilt, outspoken without blame. I have seen depressed women stay in bad relationships yet flourish, leaving depression behind. I have watched a dying woman rejoice in her life and her family rejoice in the stories she left them. I have watched the quality of writing deepen and expand. Par-

The ripples from a women's circle are not only magical, they are miraculous.

ticipants in my groups now publish: one has a contract for a television show based on her book, another's short films made it to viewing at Cannes. The circle cheers them on with the thought, *If she can, I can.* I also watch how those who move forward in craft and into publication reach back to help others along with a referral to an agent, a critique of a story. The ripples from a women's circle are not only magical, they are miraculous.

Womb of the Earth

I had not understood until I wrote this how the writing circles I lead reflect the sweat lodges I have attended. The lodge is round, symbolic of the Earth Mother. In the center is the hearth with its hot stones. Once the flap on the door is lowered, darkness descends. Prayer is offered. Ritual provides the boundaries. In turn, each person speaks from her heart (traditionally men and women attend separate lodges). Others listen. What is said is held sacred. Any response is supportive, though usually listeners only acknowledge having heard. The comparison of my groups to the sweat lodge is both accidental and archetypal. While I did not set out to use the sweat lodge model, I could not help but recreate the archetype because each women's circle reflects all such circles for all time.

Our writing is like my friend's kitchen—a hearth around which we gather a passionate collection of what matters to us. We have abundance to share—our stories, knowledge of craft, experience with publication, our tears and laughter. At a moment's notice we can pull out what is needed to assist the next woman finding her way through writing.

When we spread out our arms to include just one other woman, a circle begins to form. As we write individually and together, the changes in us are akin to our growth in childhood when we were unaware of growing until our shoes no longer fit or we saw the measurements marked on the door-jamb. Just as we grew physically through responding to the body's demands for food, water, and love, we now grow inwardly by keeping watch over the live coal in the vital, creative inner hearth. Our writing circles support and encourage us. They are the communal hearth around which we practice giving and receiving the honey of sweet acceptance.

THREE

Creative Produce

Wisdom consists in doing the next thing
that you have to do, doing it with your
whole heart and finding delight in doing it.
And the delight is the sense of the sacred.

— Helen Luke

watch a woman select produce—she presses the cantaloupe at blossom end, then sniffs. She lightly squeezes the eggplant with its smooth and shiny royal coat and dull green cap. She examines the apples for bruises and wormholes, taps the watermelon for that just-right hollow sound. The stacked oranges with their textured skin cast half moon shadows. She takes a few of these, some slender dark zucchini, and one medium tomato. I imagine her placing this bounty in a low pottery dish, pale brown and slightly rough beneath her slender fingers. She sets the dish on a wooden table in a pool of morning light. Watching her at the grocer's, I cannot decide if she will take the time to truly see what she has done, if she will recognize how she has become the Creator's hands putting the final touches on a masterpiece.

i. We Are the Water

Why is it that women disown their genius, have so much trouble claiming it, and can be swept off by the smallest current of criticism? Are we so born to pleasing others that we do not know who we are, cannot find that inner thread unless it is handed to us?

Women who bring a certain emotional openness to their writing, which many are willing to do even though they think they cannot, are the ones who let go to the writing. Only when we surrender to the writing is it free to be what we need it to be. If we push or force, then we change the course of the stream. We believe we have to remove the boulders from the stream's path, but this is not so. The water of the creative spirit finds its way around boulders or erodes them away. Our role is to honor this water, to recognize how inextricably linked to it we are—the creative spirit is not something separate from us, something we have to "get" or "learn" or "aspire to."

The water of the creative spirit resides within and expresses itself in a million ways—selecting eggplant, raising a child, preparing soup, designing a skyscraper, or leading a corporation. The purity of the expression depends on the purity of intention, and the purity of intention depends upon bringing honor to the task. By honor, I mean bringing to conscious awareness the sacred connection between Creator and creation, between creator and created. When the awareness is conscious, we honor the creative spirit by developing the discipline to study, practice, and serve through our creative gifts.

Discipline Is Not a Dirty Word

The aversion many of us have to the concept of discipline derives from its primary definition as one person's imposition of power over another through punishment. *Merriam-Webster's* second definition of the verb *discipline* is "to train or develop by instruction and exercise, esp. in self-control." A discipline is also a course of study, and a *disciple* is a student who commits to study the course. A disciple often commits to the teacher of the course of study in

This is the real curriculum for the writer: to find what best supports her writing and to do that.

order to integrate the teachings and to have someone to point the way and motivate her participation. Discipleship describes the relationship between the student and the teacher, one that creates respect, trust, and a bond of love. Love at its deepest consumes and demands sacrifice.

For a woman to create, she must sacrifice the image of what she, and possibly others, imagined her life to be. The more time she has spent conforming to an expected role, the more difficult will be the decision to claim her creative life for herself. When we feel driven to grasp our creative dream, as frequently happens in midlife, we are forced to destroy something in the old life. This may mean a divorce or a change in the division of labor; it may mean losing friends and defying traditions and socially accepted standards. It may require changing an image of ourselves as "not creative." It necessarily means that things cannot remain the same. To be remade in our own image, the old life must be destroyed. On the outside, the change may appear slight, but on the inside a new woman appears as certainly as a butterfly from a chrysalis.

Writers are disciples. Writing is both the course of study and the teacher. As disciples, we surrender to the teacher and allow ourselves to be taught. Being a writer is like committing to a graduate program with no degree or graduation date. In writing and in life, we can take simply one step at a time on a path for which we only pretend to know the destination.

Discipline demands discernment, purposeful action, and steadfastness in the face of adversity. We use our love of the teacher (writing) to build a relationship that allows us to surrender to the lessons we are given. We surrender in order to discover what our process is and to learn the skills for our craft. As a teacher, writing demands each student find the way for herself. This is the real curriculum for the writer: to find what best supports her writing and to do that.

When Writing Writes the Writer

In very practical terms, discovering our own process is the reason for writing practice. We practice writing process first and foremost, while also voraciously reading literature and nonfiction. As writers we must consume experience even when it conflicts with our personal beliefs and preferences. I have had two characters arrive on my creative doorstep who are Vietnam veterans. Writing their stories entails researching the war. I resisted the reading as long as I could because I find the subject painful. Once I began, however, I found the personal stories of the soldiers profound and enlightening. Those stories have given me a new perspective on war and soldiering, one that will deepen my characters and expand the awareness of my readers.

As part of our discipline, we practice writing in a group in order to discuss writing and refine our ability to listen critically to our own and others' work. Writing practice, strengthened by reading, discussion, and listening, builds the writing muscle that our self-confidence and our commitment can depend upon. From these experiences, we intuitively integrate the tools through which we refine our writing. Our writing becomes sensory specific, the verbs alive with action, the nouns concrete. Our characters—real or imagined—grow multidimensional and believable. With writing practice as the gym for our writing muscle, we gain the discernment to know when and what to cut, to enhance, and to let be. Books and instructors detail rules and explain point of view, rhythm, plotting, description, and so on, but nothing replaces the disciplined practice of learning by doing.

ii. Claiming the Pen

We must learn to write for ourselves first with commitment to our own expression. Only through our willingness to explore the lessons of our experience are our words able to touch anyone deeply, no matter

what we write. Life demands that
we truly experience our inner lives
in order to value them. Writing demands that we value our inner lives
before releasing them to the outer
world through our writing. Attending to these two demands—of life
and of writing—requires nurturing
our relationships with ourselves.

As a woman clarifies what matters to her, unconsciously her energy follows her thoughts and creates new experiences.

Each of us has many internalized
messages about what we can and cannot do and what we are worth. We
are led by our biology as well as acculturation to accept certain roles
and the list of "shoulds" that go with them. Women often come to
writing later in life when they can step out of biologically determined
roles and value themselves as individuals. Then, if they are willing to
also value their inner lives, they know what they have to say.

Eleanor is writing a historical novel based on family history. As she
neared the end of the first draft, her husband applauded her, innocent-
ly adding that once done she would have more time for other things,
i.e., to return to her pre-writing life in which she had more time for
him. She exploded, saying things to him she herself needed to hear:
"I am never going to stop being a writer. It is as important to me as
breathing. To hell with that other life!"

The depth of her anger frightened her (and him). I cheered her on.
She had taken an immense step toward loving herself enough to stand
up for her writing. We develop this self-love through self-care. Without
self-care, we do not feel justified in writing or in the necessary playfulness and rest that contribute to the creative process.

While we understand that we can write from the life we have lived
and find healing there, few of us consider that we can also write the

lives we might like to live. In this way, we can try them on. A third possibility also exists—that engaging in writing process results in transformation. In my ongoing Tell It Like It Is series of classes, I see the effect of finding her voice on a woman's life. By voice, I mean her particular and individual way of expressing her view of life. As a woman clarifies what matters to her, unconsciously her energy follows her thoughts and creates new experiences. More than one woman has come to class depressed over a relationship with a life partner or with her career. Over time, I notice these women grow lighter and more playful. Their writing becomes more confident and they take bigger risks. They quit apologizing for their writing.

I know a participant's story only through her writing because the class does not allow much time for socializing. Usually I learn of the change the writing has wrought after the shift has commenced. Most women stay in their partnership at home, but renegotiate their role, if not with their partner then with themselves. Several have quit jobs and struck out on new paths of self-fulfillment. Sometimes nothing in the woman's outer world changes, but she transforms how she looks at her life and that makes all the difference. I am reminded of the words of theologian and mystic Meister Eckhart: "When the soul wishes to experience something, she throws an image of the experience out before her and enters into her own image."

iii. Plotting Escape

The panoply of life guarantees us certain experiences: pain, suffering, and death. We cannot escape or control any of these, although we can choose the attitude with which we meet them. The desire to escape our pain and suffering creates resistance that enhances the pain and suffering. This cycle is universally human. By identifying the obstacles generated by our resistance, we can more easily plot a course over or through them.

Obstacle One

The first major obstacle to writing is that we believe there should not be obstacles. Even though the world teaches us otherwise, we still believe creativity and excellence do not require hard work. In contrast, we learn about the skaters and swimmers who practice six hours a day, seven days a week for years before they reach the Olympics. Even then, they may not win a medal. Whether they do or not, they keep practicing. We hear about Madeleine L'Engle whose *A Wrinkle in Time* received twenty-six rejections over two years before being published in 1962. Meanwhile, she kept writing and writing. *A Wrinkle in Time*— with well over sixty printings—and its sequels are considered classics of children's literature. Up to her death in 2007 at age eighty-eight, L'Engle was still writing.

We do not connect people like L'Engle with us. We do not want to believe Thomas Edison's dictum that "great accomplishments depend not so much on ingenuity as on hard work." We want to believe in a Santa Claus who will come each year and give us a gift whether we have been good or not.

Obstacle Two

The second obstacle to writing is that we listen to the wrong inner voice, hearing the "I can'ts" instead of the "I wills." Beginning many years ago, I had a series of dreams about claiming the guru's chair. The chair was white and sat empty on a red-carpeted dais. I stood at the

Now I see none of us "grows up." We "grow in" if we choose to grow at all, and we never come to the end of that journey, possibly not even in death.

back of the room in an auditorium filled with friends and family as well as strangers. I was told to walk down the aisle, step up on the dais, and sit in the chair. Even though I could walk down the aisle, I was physically unable to step up on the dais. Jesus appeared behind the chair and beckoned me, indicating he supported my claiming the chair. But my legs turned to stone and I could not step up. I called on angels to lift me, and though they came, they said I had to make that step myself. All they could give me was encouragement.

In my non-dream life, I was aware of a huge barrier to my lifelong desire to write and to combine writing with my love of teaching. I would move forward a few steps and hit a wall and then fall into depression and despair. *I am not good enough,* I told myself. *I do not know how.* For years I filled notebooks with descriptions of hitting the wall. Even when rereading these journals, I never gave myself credit for inching my way along the wall in search of an opening.

It took over twenty-five years for me to recover from my one unsatisfactory attempt at creative writing in college and enroll in another class. The second time I had a compassionate teacher. It did not hurt that I was one of three nontraditional students (I was over forty years old) in a class of eighteen- and nineteen-year-olds, most of whom wanted to write scripts for television adventure series. I wrote my first short story based on my experience working with the Eastern Band of Cherokee Indians. The subject was one with which I had a deep heart connection, but I could not write the story as nonfiction without breaking confidentiality. The release my soul found through fiction astounded me. I *could* do what I thought I could not. I took more classes and began teaching a class in creative journaling. I knew then I had found how to combine my two loves: teaching adults and writing.

Nevertheless, I still kept hitting the wall. With the help of a business coach, I learned that the wall was built from the rocks of negative self-talk which in turn were chips off solid blocks of a deep sense of unworthiness. Beginning in the seventies, I had participated in the Human Potential Movement in San Francisco, taken and led personal and spiritual growth groups, read the books, engaged in the therapies, and explored various spiritual paths. Self-awareness, however, necessarily comes in small pieces so we can digest it more easily. As a child I thought I would not grow up because I would die young. Now I see none of us "grows up." We "grow in" if we choose to grow at all, and we never come to the end of that journey, possibly not even in death.

It took at least eight years for me to claim writing and teaching as my gifts, to recognize that what I had been seeking was within me. If I quit beating myself up and allowed myself the continual process of learning to write and learning to teach, then there was no place to go, no goal to obtain. I could sit in the white chair on the dais and claim my place in my own life.

I would like to report that this revelation came with crashing thunder, but it did not. In fact, I cannot say when it happened. I only recognized it when, thumbing through my old journals and rereading those pages of despair about hitting the wall, I realized I no longer related to the story. The wall had crumbled or I had climbed over it. I visualized the auditorium with its red-carpeted dais. I saw the chair, and I saw Jesus standing behind it. I saw myself stride down the aisle, step up, and sit down. Even now, describing this vision brings tears to my eyes and fills my heart with awe.

Obstacle Three

Another obstacle to writing is the belief that the obstacle and the answer to removing it lie outside us. I know now that the wall I kept facing was belief in my innate inferiority. I had integrated the culture that devalues women's work and extrapolated it to everything I did, believing that anything I could do easily and well had no value. I was so accustomed to being out-reasoned by intellectual virtuosity and demeaned for my intuition that I could not believe I had anything to say that anyone wanted to hear. I thought I was looking for an answer in a class or book that would tell me how to write, but I discovered I was looking for the faith in myself that would allow me to trust and value what I wrote. Underneath it all, I was terrified of being judged and criticized, not for my words as much as for who I was to have written them.

I thought I was looking for an answer in a class or book that would tell me how to write, but I discovered I was looking for the faith in myself that would allow me to trust and value what I wrote.

Embracing the Obstacles

Now that I have worked many years with women writers, both neophyte and seasoned, I know the beliefs I held are shared by many and are used to create reasons not to write. In the following table, I list common unsupportive thoughts held by women. I believe almost any other unsupportive thought can be reframed as one of these. The underlying belief is the same for all.

As women, we are vulnerable, physically and emotionally. Many of

The Thought	The Underlying Belief
I'm not creative. I'm not good enough. I don't have time. I don't know what to say. It's been said. I don't know how to start or proceed. No one would want to read what I write.	The illusion of safety is more important than discovering my truth, giving it voice, and risking revelation and rejection.

us marry and/or choose secure careers in order to create an illusion of safety. Western culture promotes the belief that security and safety are possible, especially through the accumulation of material wealth and a network of relationships, whereas individual and historical experience proves the inevitability of change and the vulnerability of human life. As a friend with breast cancer pointed out, "At any moment your life can change. I walked in the doctor's office healthy and walked out with a life-threatening illness." The inevitability of change is the truth of life and the reason safety is an illusion.

Being a writer requires recognizing our vulnerability while sustaining faith in ourselves. Vulnerability can generate fear, while faith in our own courage allows us to be fearless. Fearlessness does not equal recklessness. Fearlessness brings the recognition that fear is not a wall, but a feeling of anxiety that is also akin to excitement and anticipation. We can choose to see fear as the harbinger of possibility instead of danger.

iv. Finding Faith in Dark Places

Faith is not the opposite of doubt; it is a tiny seed in the heart about our place in the basic nature of things. The soul, our true self, has no beliefs, only faith. Faith is a knowing, a oneness with something whether we see it or not. Faith is in the present moment, yet it increases with our experience. We have faith the sun will rise each day because our experience reinforces our faith.

On every heroic journey, faith is challenged.

Deep inside every woman who wants to write exists a seed of faith that she can do it or she would not entertain the possibility. Somewhere and somehow this faith in herself germinated. Perhaps it has been buried under a rubbish pile of self-doubt, but the fact that the desire is present is proof that the faith is still alive. We do not have to generate faith, but we do need to expand it through experience, the experience of writing itself. As we write, we develop enough faith to seek the support of others. We look for at least one person whom we respect to affirm our faith.

On every heroic journey, faith is challenged. Even Jesus wrestled with the devil. I had just found the person who affirmed my writing, and was filled with the possibility of claiming my chair, when I was confronted with my own dark knight. My friend Donna invited me to one of her monthly gatherings. The intent of this particular meeting was to allow participants to speak dreams they wanted to manifest in their lives. I remember the trepidation I felt as I stepped into the open-air pavilion and sat on the unfinished wood floor. Fifteen people gathered in a circle and settled into silence. The river below us and the birds in the surrounding trees chanted an accompaniment to our meditation. I spent the time imagining myself saying, "I am a writer. I am determined to commit to learning my craft." The women and men present did not know how monumental and terrifying this statement seemed to me. They did not know how much courage I had mustered in order to attend. I could still pass when my turn came, but I knew I would not. This felt like my one chance. Not voicing my dream would be a defeat from which I might never recover.

After meditation, when my turn came, I spoke with sureness and I was heard. My heart sang louder than the river and birds. I wanted to jump up and dance, to shout, *Yes! I CAN do this, I AM a writer.* I was so certain.

When the circle was over we gathered in Donna's house for a pot-luck. Kay was there too. She, Donna, and I were members of a small women's spiritual leadership group. They were the poles of the group, Donna soft, accepting, and romantic, with a strong inner spirit, and Kay, bold and intellectual, poised for action. Donna led sweat lodges and meditation groups. Kay led communications workshops in which she emphasized the need to monitor one's speech to expunge any negativity.

Kay was present when another woman commented to me that she had felt the passion behind my statement of intention and that she supported me. Thanking her, I said, "I decided that this is something I have to do before I die."

"Don't say that!" Kay said, her tone angry and demanding.

I felt my body close in on itself, and the other woman spoke, "Yes, you shouldn't say it that way because then if you do write, you might die."

I wanted to laugh at this bizarre reasoning, but I was still reeling from Kay's command. Though it was difficult, I managed to speak, struggling to redeem myself and reawaken the joy I had reveled in just moments before. "In one Native American tradition, a warrior greeted the sun every morning by saying, 'This would be a good day to die.' This is what I meant—to remind myself to follow my dream totally today so I won't die with my gifts ungiven."

I do not recall if any conversation followed that. I tried to eat, but could not. At last I decided I had to leave, or I would either weep or scream the pain that was reverberating through me from the words, "Don't say that."

As I said goodbye to Donna, Kay came to the door. I knew I had to acknowledge what had happened. "Your words opened an old wound, Kay," I said. "I don't understand why, but you need to know they devastated me." I didn't wait for her reply.

In my car on the thirty-mile drive home, I wept and screamed and pounded the steering wheel. By the time I arrived my hand was bruised and my throat raw. I could not remember ever having such a reaction to someone's words. For the next three days, I sat in a chair weeping, writing, and trying to find the reason for my reaction. I could acknowledge that Kay's demand reflected her own fears and that the wound she had opened was not one she had inflicted. Whatever had caused it originally, this message of "Don't say that!" spoken in an authoritarian voice was at the heart of my fear about my writing. I was also responsible. In the excitement of having permission to pursue my writing, I exposed my fragile dream to the world. Instead of nurturing its roots, I pulled it out of its protective soil to show it off.

I could not—and still cannot—ferret out the origin of the wound. I recall various incidents in my life where I was punished or shamed for speaking out. In other instances, I asked for support or validation for my opinions or my writing and either received none or was criticized. No single memory is accompanied by a "that's it" feeling. At the time of this writing, I experienced the re-opening of the wound in another incident in which my husband corrected my wording of a declaration of intent for my business. Actually, he had misunderstood the declaration. In the much-ado-about-nothing aftermath, my wound re-opened, leaving me raw.

In both instances, three components existed: I perceived that a trusted confidante had imposed her or his will on me. The message I heard was that I am neither entitled to choose my words nor to seek fulfillment of my dreams; and I experienced the imposition of these messages as psychic attacks.

The origin of the wound is not as important as identifying it and acknowledging its impact on my creative life. While this wound had held me back from my writing for years, it had also acted to nourish my interest in spiritual and personal healing and growth and pushed me toward learning how to facilitate individuals and groups. Unsure of my place in the outer world, I developed a rich inner life. Kay's words acted unconsciously to synthesize my educational and life experiences with my gifts of teaching adults and writing. This synthesis morphed into a passion for supporting women in developing their voice and expressing it through writing.

From Kay's words I learned to be more circumspect about when and with whom to share my aspirations. I saw clearly how dependent I was on the approval of others, allowing them to encourage or discourage me in almost every area of my life. I sometimes forget to couple my intuition with discernment in order to learn from my critics without letting them

Protecting our faith in ourselves requires vigilance in the present moment because that is where faith exists.

challenge my basic truth. This was the reminder I received from my husband—I reacted emotionally based on childhood experience before discerning that he had misheard what I said.

I tell this story because few of us have had supportive and positive responses to our creative efforts. We carry hurts, and each hurt has its trigger. To write, we have to ferret out our wounds and make their acquaintance. Each one comes with gifts as well as pain. Each one reminds us that no matter what we have been told, we still have that little seed of faith within that says we can write. For that seed to grow, we must accept total responsibility for its care and nurturance.

People, events, or our own negative thought patterns can threaten our faith and drive it underground unless we remain aware and alert. Protecting our faith in ourselves requires vigilance in the present moment because that is where faith exists. If we stand on faith and project into the future, we move from faith to hope, from attention in the present to expectation for the future.

When I first read Buddhist teacher Pema Chodron's suggestion that her students might hang the sign "Abandon Hope" above their doorways, I resisted. Giving up hope means giving up. Or, does it?

While exploring the teaching, I discovered that if I maintained my attention on nurturing my faith by taking the next step in my writing each day, I grew in assurance. If I lapsed into hoping about what the writing would become and what would happen to it in the future, I drained my energy from the work of the moment. Dwelling on hope also opened the door to the messages of self-doubt: *it cannot happen, I am not good enough,* and so on.

The dictionary defines *hope* as "to desire with expectation of obtainment or to trust by expecting with confidence." Most of us, however, use "I hope" with a dose of doubt thrown in. I have chosen to abandon hope and focus on faith by addressing the next step of the work at hand each moment. This approach builds trust within myself and keeps the demons of self-doubt away.

v. I Accept!

While sitting in the chair of our lives brings with it responsibility
and risk, it also necessitates accepting acknowledgement and praise.
In my classes, almost all new members go through a period in which
they apologize and excuse their work. Over time, they learn two things:
first, that when read, the piece does not sound as bad as they antici-
pated, and second, that they—not their listeners—are the ones holding
the yardstick.

One participant sat through six weeks of classes without reading. No one is required to read, but she was the first and only person
to hold out for so long. I finally asked to speak to her individually. I
learned that she suffered from debilitating shyness. She could not even
read one of her pieces to me when we were alone. I asked if I could
read to her if she picked out the piece. Once she heard it from someone else's mouth, she accepted that her writing was as good as any she
had heard in class. At the final class, she read at every opportunity and
received accolades from class members.

Several years ago I was asked to speak at the annual celebratory
convention of an inner-city ministry. The congregation was led by a
woman who had developed a program to provide the marginalized—
drug dealers and users, prostitutes, the poor, destitute, homeless, and
jobless—with the self-confidence and inspiration needed to change
their lives. I never would have guessed their pasts when I met the
congregants in the dining room and talked with them in the halls. The
place reverberated with joy from these well-spoken, well-dressed, self-
motivated, and enthusiastic people.

I noticed that when they passed in the hall, they greeted one
another with, "God bless you, I love you." I also observed that whenever anyone received a compliment or a positive suggestion, even as

offhand as "Nice dress" or "Maybe you'll win the lottery," the recipient responded with an enthusiastic, "I accept!"

I tell this story often and encourage women to practice saying "I accept!" at every opportunity. Learning to own our abilities without comparing them to those of others increases our confidence, deepens the pleasure of life experiences, and enhances our writing. We begin to notice the tendency to qualify our work with words like *but, however, may, perhaps,* and *just.* Writing, however, is about taking a firm stand, whether through poetry, fiction, or nonfiction. We develop the confidence to take the heat from those who disagree.

I return to the woman in the produce section who selected her vegetables with the care Cézanne might have taken in composing a still life. Now, she lifts the eggplant and the tomato from the pottery bowl, washes them, and sets them on a cutting board. She picks up a knife, its blade catching the afternoon light from the open window. She slices the eggplant into large coins of creamy flesh, each coin ringed by purple and containing an inner circlet of brown seeds. She transforms the tomato from globe to wedges. Spring onions and cloves of garlic, stripped of their dull skins, glow like white and green pearls. Next, the orange, round and pebbly in her hand, meets the knife's edge. Inside, the perfectly divided segments with their striations of white harbor teardrop seeds and a juicy sweetness almost overwhelming in its perfume.

She performs such alchemy daily, automatically perhaps. Even if she stays aware of the essence of what she sees and tastes and smells and does, she may not be aware of a deep teaching about comparison.

Is the eggplant more beautiful whole or when it is sliced on the cutting board or browned in a skillet? Who can compare segmenting an orange with slicing it? Is the eggplant better than the orange? Although we may have a preference for oranges, ours is not the only preference and could not stand up in argument with someone who loves eggplant. Is a Cézanne better than a Matisse or a Rembrandt?

Awareness is the key, being present to what is, writing from the juicy innards of awareness, always toward that complete sphere of wholeness we yearn to express.

We fail, by the way. The story or book, like our mother's recipe for eggplant parmigiana, never becomes quite the perfection we have imagined. And, if it did, might we be afraid to try again?

FOUR

Our Lady Underground

Metaphor is the language of the soul. Through a physical
image, metaphor reveals a spiritual truth or condition.
Take, for example, a line from a Zen koan: "Hide yourself
in the middle of the flames." . . . if we understand metaphor
at all . . . we understand we're being challenged to risk all in
our passion for life, and our cells shout yes. Just as metaphor
encompasses spirit and body, so, as I use the term, soul is
the meeting place of spirit and body, the eternal part of
us that lives in the body while we are on Earth. Soul
is traditionally feminine in both men and women.

— Marion Woodman

*O*utside *Chartres Cathedral of Notre Dame, three women, dressed in black, red, and white folk costumes, sit at a table bathed with soft autumn sunshine. I watch their hands flutter like winter birds across the lace boards. Confined to woman's work, their ancestral mothers could not be confined to the plain and ordinary stitches of mending and patching. They were driven to create lace as extraordinary in its vulnerable delicacy as the monumental solidity of the cathedral made by men.*

Inside the dark nave, cool silence echoes the voice of God the mother. While others stand peering upward at arched ribs and rose window, I make my way to Our Lady of the Pillar, a statue of the Black Madonna. Another Black Madonna, Our Lady Underground, resides in the earth's womb beneath me. I feel the dark mother's energy pulling me into her rich, moist cave. For all the comfort she offers, I sense she will strip me clean through painful passages. My yearning is strong, and I am young. Before leaving, I seal my fate by walking the labyrinth, laboring over my slow steps inward, deep into my soul, soul of woman, asking to be reborn in her image.

i. The Web of the Feminine

For all its seeming fragility, lace is strong, like a spider's web, like the many seemingly transitory and invisible works of women through generations. Babies and businesses birthed, the growing of crops and rearing of children, meals and corpses laid out—all comprise the web women weave to hold the world together. Despite subjugation, derision, and exclusion from the decisions affecting them, women find ways to survive.

Claiming the fullness of the feminine requires fully exploring and integrating all the feminine archetypes as parts of ourselves.

Every woman, whether consciously or not, carries within her the many aspects of an overarching feminine archetype I call Lord Mother. These aspects include the archetypes we readily acknowledge: the maiden, queen, mother, and crone or wise woman, and those less acknowledged: the hag with her spells and potions, the seductress, the wicked mother, and the lesser-known Black Madonna.

Artistic renditions of the Black Madonna have been present in Catholic traditions for at least a thousand years. Our Lady of Guadalupe (Mexico) and Our Lady of Czestochowa (Poland) are the most familiar examples. The image transcends race and ethnicity, but centuries of racism have contributed to interpretations of her as a negative feminine archetype. She is also feared because she symbolizes challenges to existing standards through honest speech and decisive action. The Black Madonna is now re-emerging around the world in women's dreams, visions, and artwork. Women express her energy when they dare to break with societal rules and traditions in order to effect positive change, especially in support of liberation, equality, and justice for the disenfranchised and for the preservation of the earth.

We women have survived by developing our pure, nurturing sides, while keeping hag, seductress, wicked mother, and Black Madonna hidden, even from ourselves. We have been taught that these archetypes are the dangerous ones, the powerful, fiery, sensual, and truthful ones for which women have been punished, the ones embodied by the "witches" of Salem and the Inquisition who were killed for their use of herbal medicine, their intuitive powers, and because men lusted for them. We have lost count of the many women imprisoned or casti-gated for speaking out for social justice, women's rights, and child labor laws. These women represent the sides of the feminine we deny—she whose sharp claws and fangs will stop at nothing to protect those she loves. Like the Hindu goddess Kali, they illustrate the ability of Lord Mother to destroy in order to create, whether through new laws, new social structures, or new works of art and literature.

Claiming the fullness of the feminine requires fully exploring and integrating all the feminine archetypes as parts of ourselves. Without the power and wisdom they bring us, without their insight into both our darkness and our light, we cannot stand alone on our own terms. As long as we shrink from their challenge to be totally ourselves, we will not have the freedom to create.

No wonder we are afraid to write.

ii. Soul-Making

Creativity is necessarily soul work. The soul is the province of the feminine principle within both genders. The soul is driven to share itself in a manner that makes a difference in the world. The soul's work is a process of winnowing out all that is not a true expression of itself. This process can be seen as our destiny. We each have certain gifts, opportunities, and experiences we can use to learn the lessons of our soul's journey. We also have free will, so if, when, and what we learn are always choices. Soul work or "Soul-making," as the poet John Keats called it, inspires creativity, in the act of which spirit and matter join to make whole.

Creativity always comes from the inside, the center of our being, and moves out toward manifestation. This inner-to-outer movement parallels a movement from self-expression and the world of the personality toward the expression of the universal, the Self with that capital S. The more we practice writing, the more often our small selves and small minds step aside to make room for the revelation of Self or Big Mind. At such moments, the feeling of the heart meets the discernment of the mind and comes into physical form through an action of the body. Words, paint, and music flow; the clay takes shape; the dance is lifted from a series of steps to a transformation of music into movement. Inspirited, we truly express our souls—in art, work, relationships, and in service. While the soul is the province of the feminine, its work is the synthesis of feminine and masculine energies.

More and more, contemporary women risk revealing the feminine images and symbolism of their thoughts and dreams through their creative expression. In recent years women's spiritual poetry long archived in museum storerooms—Hildegard of Bingen, Sappho, Pan Zhao, and others—has appeared in translation on bookstore shelves. From the time of the women's movement in the 1970s, women's poetry, stories, plays, and novels have cut ever closer to the bone of women's physical experience. Adrienne Rich's poem "Rape" (1973) and Eve Ensler's play *The Vagina Monologues* (1998) are examples.

The influence of goddess and earth religions, paganism and indigenous spiritual practices, and ancient Eastern symbols along with more classic themes, increasingly pervade the art of women. The artists' willingness to share their inner lives expands the collective feminine energy and is giving birth to a feminine consciousness never before fully realized in human history. We do not know what full realization of this energy might mean, only that women are being called toward its embodiment by one another and by male spiritual leaders such as Bishop Tutu, the Hopi elders, and Father Matthew Fox. A few of the women speaking and modeling this embodiment include Jungians

Currently the Western world is confused about terms, equating feminine energy with women and masculine energy with men, whereas each gender possesses both feminine and masculine energies and archetypes.

Marion Woodman, Jean Shinoda Bolen, and Clara Pinkola Estés, writers Belle Hooks and Maya Angelou, and Nobel Peace Prize recipients Shirin Ebadi (Iran, 2003) and Wangari Muta Maathai (Kenya, 2004).

In understanding the feminine, we understand the masculine. One does not exist without the other any more than light exists without shadow. Currently the Western world is confused about terms, equating feminine energy with women and masculine energy with men, whereas each gender possesses both feminine and masculine energies and archetypes. Many women hold men responsible for the ascendancy of the Power Principle, also called the patriarchy. Fueled by greed and the lust for power and ruled by fear, the Power Principle rapes both genders. What has happened to our societies and the earth has been condoned to some degree by all of us, women and men.

As Marion Woodman points out, the soul is traditionally feminine in both men and women. Women have moved further in integrating the masculine than men have in integrating their feminine side. As a result, women can access the soul more directly and easily than men. Currently, men are far more trapped by the Power Principle than women. Comparatively liberated, we are called upon to recognize men's plight and to lead the way with our individual soul-making. We can model the embodiment of the synthesis of masculine and feminine energies. In this way, we will meet Thomas Banyacya's challenge to take responsibility for the table of the earth and Bishop Tutu's challenge to unleash our power in order to transform the economic, social, and political institutions of the world.

iii. Yin and Yang

A Chinese friend from Taiwan expanded my understanding of the feminine and masculine as energy with this explanation of the Taoist concept of yin-yang.

"Yin-yang," he told me, "provides a way of looking at the world as inclusive and whole. Look at a quarter." He pulled one from his pocket. "This side is heads, this side is tails; but neither side is the quarter. The quarter lies between the two. Yin-yang. Two sides, same coin." He grinned and, because he loves metaphor as much as I, said, "Or, you can imagine a river. A river begins as a stream, placid and slow. That's yin. Then maybe there're some rapids and a waterfall. That's yang. But at the bottom of the waterfall there's a deep quiet pool. That's yin again. So there's this movement from yin to yang and back to yin, over and over. But it's all the same river."

When we see the symbol for yin-yang, we see a static circle, half white and half black. We may fail to notice that within the white is a black circle and within the black a white one. We forget entirely to imagine that the larger circle is in flux, always changing. The line between yin and yang in the symbol is perfectly curved, and if extended would become the symbol of a wave, the unending rhythmic flow of balanced energy.

Yin encompasses the feminine and the soul, the moon, and the qualities of softness, darkness, flexibility, receptivity, nurturance, and intuition. Because the feminine represents the earth and the body, it is attuned to cycles of matter, such as birth-death and creation-destruction.

Yang encompasses the masculine, the sun, and the qualities of hardness, light, strength, reason, and expression. The masculine represents spirit, inspiring through penetration and acting linearly toward a goal.

The power of the yin-yang concept lies in the understanding that each of the opposites contains the other, that all things are comprised of yin and yang. The cyclical flow from one to the other ensures that when balanced, one never dominates, except temporarily. The masculine without the feminine, Jungian analyst Marion Woodman says, is a ghost (spirit without matter); the feminine without the masculine is a corpse (matter without spirit). By embracing the yin/ yang, the misperception that the world is either/or passes away, and the reality of both/and, in which feminine and masculine are synthesized, manifests.

By embracing the yin/ yang, the misperception that the world is either/ or passes away, and the reality of both/and, in which feminine and masculine are synthesized, manifests.

In creativity, yin is process, yang is product. Process, the play of the unconscious grounded through the body, is the soil in which the product germinates. The seed of the product is in the inspiration (masculine) and receptivity to the intuition (feminine) that begins the creative process. Through gestation and experimentation, inspiration and intuition dance together until, little by little, imagination leads the creator into evolving an expressive form. The form thus created can be thought of as inspirited matter— the synthesis of masculine and feminine.

For many women writers, being receptive to intuition requires opening the gate to possibility and playing with words and images.

The clarity of a writer's voice is dependent on the degree of her willingness to delve into the darkness of her own being and the darkness of the world as she experiences it.

An image eventually grabs the pen and begins to lead the way; this is the inspiration toward form. If enough energy exists toward exploration, the writer dances between exploring the process and entertaining the possibility of product until finally a draft of a form emerges as poem, memoir, essay, story. There are points in this dance in which product and process intersect, carrying the writer to that place where masculine and feminine, human and divine, ethereal and mundane become one. Time and place disappear. We become as Michelangelo with his marble, in a state of focused ecstasy, carefully removing all that is not the poem or prose until the crafted piece is revealed. My poet friend Randal Pride gave me the term for this: the transcendence of craft. Once experienced, writers seek this transcendent soulful point. The true art of writing lies within, dancing on the tip of the pen.

iv. Four Wisdoms for Writers

As the archetypal feminine, Lord Mother offers teachings that are classrooms for the individual soul work essential to our creative journeys. In fact, her primary message asks that we create and give birth to a new way of being in this world. Each teaching is a sacred wisdom she wishes us to learn and practice. I have distilled these wisdoms into four to show how each relates to our writing. Through the four wisdoms we can better understand how writing gradually and gently unwraps us to reveal our souls, and how the process of writing itself informs our progress through our lives and heals and helps us on our way.

The Wisdom of Not Knowing

The clarity of a writer's voice is dependent on the degree of her willingness to delve into the darkness of her own being and the darkness of the world as she experiences it. She faces herself squarely with a spirit of curiosity, adventure, and an openness to not knowing what she will find. The Wisdom of Not Knowing urges us to trust the truth of Carl Jung's observation that our shadow side hides, not some terrible depravity, but our unidentified and unrealized potential. Once recognized and refined, the darkness reveals itself as 90 percent gold. For the writer, this is proven by the truth she is willing to put upon the page. The deeper the writer is willing to go within herself, the more profound will be the effect of her words.

Digging into the darkness to write does not mean that the writing itself must be ponderous, serious, or dark in nature. Humor provides the best case in point. We laugh when the humorist strikes a raw chord that makes us uncomfortable. When we dare to delve into our personal darkness, we find those places where our individual experiences touch collective experience. We discover the myths and the archetypes of our particular culture at a particular time. Like any artist, the humorist touches our vulnerability because she has touched her own. The role of the artist requires exposing personal vulnerability: that is the price of admission for making art.

During a time of deep self-searching, I had a dream in which I was invited into a cave to stand, surrounded by other women, before a crystal altar. I understood that any offering had to be total. I was required to give all of myself, leaving nothing out. I held back. I wanted to give only my "goodness" while hiding my "bad" parts in the folds of my skirt. Deeper integration of the dream came later when I understood that offering all of myself meant recognizing all parts of myself—mind, spirit, soul, and body—as sacred. I had to be willing to be unequivocally *me*, not the *persona* I had learned to project. This challenge propelled me deeper into my own heroic journey.

Because the feminine is characteristically responsive, women have an innate capacity to tolerate waiting and the *not knowing* that waiting demands. Having the capacity does not mean we embrace it. When my friend Father Frank understood he would die from his cancer, he told me, "Just because I'm not afraid to die, doesn't mean I want to do it!" This is true for many of us with writing. We want to write because we have written and touched the joy-filled spaciousness. While the joy of writing lures us in, the Wisdom of Not Knowing reminds us that to create is to destroy. If we are to be writers, we are forced to submit to our own annihilation. If we love the truth enough to seek it out, we agree to live with uncertainty and discomfort, to quit pretending that safety and security are possible in this world. Fear is an inevitable fellow traveler on the creative journey. When fear settles next to us, it alerts us to possibility and growth.

Like the pull of the moon on the tide, Lord Mother calls to us, insisting we wake up and speak. Millions of women hear this call as a

If we are to be writers, we are forced to submit to our own annihilation. If we love the truth enough to seek it out, we agree to live with uncertainty and discomfort, to quit pretending that safety and security are possible in this world.

call to creativity, particularly to writing. It is as though our souls, pent up and starved for generations, refuse further containment. Frightened though we often are of what this energetic surge might reveal, we begin taking the risk, bolstered by the company of other women.

The fear this heroic endeavor engenders is akin to grief. When someone dear to us dies, we discover that much of how we have defined ourselves was a reflection of how we were seen by this other. Without the reflection we become disoriented and ungrounded; life loses its touchstones for meaning. Likewise, when a part of us shows signs of ebbing away, we question everything we have thought about ourselves. We do not know what we will have to give up to birth what is calling us from within. We do not know who of those we love will stand by us through the process.

We cannot write well by staying on the surface of our lives or by attempting to hide our true selves behind our words. The Wisdom of Not Knowing challenges us to truth telling. It sends us into the mines to chip away at all the layers concealing the gold of ourselves. It challenges us to bring our precious metal to the light and return to the depths for more. Mining our selves, our lives, is not a one-time thing. We free the pen to dig deep whenever we pick it up. This is how writing heals us and how it makes us whole. This is why writing excites and energizes and nourishes us. This is also why writing scares us.

The Wisdom of the Ecology of Body and Earth

Lord Mother is Creatrix of Life and Cosmic Mother. The word *mother* in Latin is *mater,* meaning matter. The Wisdom of Ecology teaches us the interconnectedness of all things. It teaches that every bit of matter has an ecosystem that is interdependent with every other. This is as true of the earth as it is of the anthill and as true of the anthill as it is of the human body. Lord Mother pulls us downward into our bodies to the lower centers of energy—those that concern personal power, creativity, and sexuality.

Women unconsciously connect to the physical senses that inform their sensuality, to the cycles of nature in the earth (seasons, moon phases, tides), and in their bodies (menses, birth-life-death). As writers, these connections ground our work, informing our symbols and metaphors and providing themes.

To develop her writing voice, a woman's centers of creativity and personal power must be open. Western culture has cut us off at the waist, so that we operate primarily from our heads. This truncation effectively severs communication between the centers of intellect, communication, and compassion in the upper body and the centers of power, creativity, and sexuality in the lower body. Over generations, women have been debased and abused around issues of copulation, conception and childbirth, so we should not be surprised when we have difficulty claiming our creative power. The instinct to stay in our heads within the safe restraints imposed on us, however, can prove as dangerous as taking the risk of stepping into the totality of our being.

At a time of crisis when I felt pulled apart by the overwhelming demands on my time and energy, I had a significant dream. I watched a young woman lead a cougar on a leash into a clearing. From the edge of the forest a large black bear ran toward the cat.

"Let go of the leash!" I yelled, knowing that if the woman did not let go, she risked her own life as well as the cougar's.

She did not release the leash, and a horrible fight between bear and cougar ensued. The animals soon disappeared, and she was left lying on the ground. From a service station where I had run for help, men rushed to her aid. I watched as an ambulance took her away, uncertain if she would survive.

The young woman in the dream symbolizes me and all women. She illustrates how we restrain our feminine power to create and thereby risk its destruction by overdeveloping our maternal impulse to help, nurture, and serve others. To move into maturity and live fully from our unfettered power, we let go of restraint, stand in our power, and defend our right to creative expression. We also remember to go to a "service station" for help, to fuel our own tank, and to seek support for our healing.

In some Eastern constructs of the body's energetic system, the personal power center resides within the lower torso in the area behind the navel, while the creative power center lies in the womb space in the lower abdomen. Breathing into the belly aligns these two centers, allowing body and being to relax and expand. This alignment between the personal power center and the creative power center allows us to take the flexible stance inherent to our feminine nature.

Voice in writing arises from centered power. Voice has authority. Voice is the author speaking clearly and individually without equivocation or apology.

Ecological relationships are fluid, like yin-yang. Nature is always in flux, even at the atomic and cellular levels. The Power Principle depends on dualistic thinking, a world of opposites. In such a construct, change evokes rigidity and resistance rather than flexibility and fluidity. Lord Mother teaches that change and ambiguity are inevitable; she begs us to embrace them.

We express the knowing of the belly through our voice, actual and metaphorical. Voice in writing arises from centered power. Voice has authority. Voice is the author speaking clearly and individually without equivocation or apology.

The Wisdom of the Ecology of Body and Earth teaches us to accept and embrace the feminine's inclination to exert power through relationships and responsiveness. These inclinations are strengths, not weaknesses. A woman does not need to will herself toward a goal like a soldier on the battleground, nor does she need the enticement of prestige or domination in order to serve and nurture. The feminine energy within us desires instead to create life as a safe space in which to respond intuitively from the heart. Responsiveness brings the creative gift of extending ourselves meaningfully and individually with true feeling.

A woman's heroic journey can be summarized as her search for the ecological relationship between her creative responsiveness and her intense desire to create something in matter that is uniquely hers, something that sings of her soul across time.

The shadow side of responsiveness often reveals itself in an absence of boundaries and in resentment and overwhelm at feeling responsible for the care and happiness of others. The word *ecology* in this wisdom reminds us that part of our lesson is to seek a proper relationship between others and ourselves. In this way, we will become response-able *with* others rather than responsible *for* them.

Our identities as women, even if we are also business owners or soldiers, are still very much tied to relationships with others. We want to serve, to help, and to nurture, both within and outside our homes. The mindful attention we bring daily to situations by creating a space for comfort and nurturance is a creative expression of the sacred feminine. Because feminine responsiveness does not make the splash or the money and success required in our culture, because it is not "out there" and "in your face," women, as well as men, devalue it.

By the 1970s the Power Principle had co-opted the women's movement, opening the doors to women on condition that they turn their backs on their roles as nurturers and responders and become competitive and action-driven. With few models for feminine power based on the synthesis of feminine and masculine, we went to where the power lay—into the world of the Power Principle. Now is the time of redefinition of feminine power, a definition based on inner values rather than on outer roles and actions.

A woman's heroic journey can be summarized as her search for the ecological relationship between her creative responsiveness and her intense desire to create something *in matter* that is uniquely hers, something that sings of her soul across time. We yearn to externally manifest our internal experience in a form that reflects, yet is apart from, our relationships with others.

The feminine moves from the inside out and from individual to collective. To write, to create any art purely for our own joy and nurturance, requires examining and prioritizing the relationship with ourselves and setting boundaries for our relationships with others. Many women feel selfish when they take this step and are often harshly judged by their peers. Lord Mother sees no virtue in self-denial. She asks us to examine what rewards we perceive we are receiving when we renounce the experience of our own joy. Are we seeking the sympathy allotted to a martyr? The safety of keeping our wings untested? The certain approval derived from encouraging others to be dependent on us?

Lord Mother also challenges us to nurture the creative power within us, to trust it and to follow its lead without reining it in. She asks us to nurture and care for the earth, and to go to nature for the lessons of ecological interdependence. As we listen to these lessons, we find our own seasons for planting, blossoming, reaping, and for lying fallow. We find here our individual answers to honoring our creativity in all its manifestations and to accepting all of these as of equal value to ourselves and to humanity.

The Wisdom of Fierce Compassion

A term used by author China Galland, "fierce compassion" means not averting our gaze. As long as we avert our gaze from what pains our hearts and minds, we protect ourselves from responsibility as well as from response-ability.

Compassion means shared suffering, a condition of the heart. Compassion does not necessitate any action beyond the extension of love, although action motivated by pure compassion heals. "Helping" is the shadow of compassion and creates a hierarchical relationship between those empowering and those being empowered. Women like to think of helping others—especially the disenfranchised, ill, and weak. Unfortunately, their motives may include showing their own superiority by reaching "down" to help someone else "up," in which case they are imposing their power on others. Compassion, not helping, is embodied feminine power—a way to do by being present that does not necessarily require an outer action.

Fierce compassion has two components we often interpret as antithetical to one another: power and empathy. Over centuries women have grown accustomed to being at the mercy of power, of deferring to masculine power, and to feeling *power-less*. Most of us, men and women, do not truly understand what power feels like when it is not defined by a hierarchical relationship to others. Lord Mother insists that, as women, we discover and redefine power in terms of our relationship with ourselves first. Clarification of this relationship changes our energetic power in relation to others.

Historically, masculine power was assumed because physical strength enabled men to both protect and subjugate those with less strength. Power Principle societies portray power in women as a negative expression of the feminine. A powerful woman is cast as a shrew, a pushy broad, a bitch, or at best, a lonely and unfulfilled person. Women and men alike too often promote the image of the somewhat helpless, sweet, and nurturing woman even while women build airplanes, run companies, take political office, and command space shuttles.

Fierce compassion can be understood as the synthesis of the heart of love in the chest cavity with the heart of creativity in the womb cavity expressing through the individual's personal power as True Power.

Lord Mother shows us that compassion and power are not antithetical, that these two forces nurture and impassion one another. Fierce compassion can be understood as the synthesis of the heart of love in the chest cavity with the heart of creativity in the womb cavity expressing through the individual's personal power as True Power. True Power is not wielded but shared. True Power communicates *power to* rather than *power over*. *Power to* begets influence that enlists cooperation and generates dialogue and communication. *Power over* creates resistance, the foundation for violence, and is the progenitor of rhetoric and dogma.

The power that women innately hold confounds thought. The nineteenth-century poet Matthew Arnold wrote, "If ever there comes a time when the women of the world come together purely and simply for the benefit of [hu]mankind, it will be a force such as the world has never seen." Most confounding is that many of us women do not accept that we hold such power. We are slaves to a history of helplessness and afraid to venture beyond the safety of what we know. Certainly risk exists. Those men well known for expressing feminine qualities through their compassion, messages of peace, and intuitive wisdom have shown us the danger: Jesus of Nazareth, Mahatma Gandhi, Thich Nhat Hanh, Martin Luther King, and Nelson Mandela, among many.

There is no doubt that a pen wielded by a thoughtful woman can change history.

Whenever a new force wishes to be manifested, it appears first in art of all kinds. The written word has tremendous power. Fueled by fierce compassion, we allow the pen to change us. Once we learn to follow the pen's lead, we enter a symbiotic relationship with our writing so that, as we are changed, so are our thoughts and words. There is no doubt that a pen wielded by a thoughtful woman can change history. We remember Harriet Beecher Stowe, Virginia Woolf, Rachel Carson, and Audre Lorde to mention only a few.

For us to learn the Wisdom of Fierce Compassion requires looking at our own foibles and at the human condition without flinching. Fierce compassion does not turn its back on either suffering or joy. When we reveal ourselves through our writing and do not turn away, we connect with the reader and impact lives. The genre in which we write does not matter as long as our writing comes from this centered power point. Fierce compassion does not mean we must take up overt social action, only that we *do not avert our gaze.*

I have met many women who refuse to listen, watch, or read the news because of the violence and suffering portrayed. I went through a period like this myself until I realized I was trying to pretend that I was not connected to the people to whom bad things happened. By averting my gaze, I could not honor the slain and injured civilians and soldiers, the tsunami victims, the starving refugees across the world. By averting my gaze, I was avoiding my responsibility as a citizen of the world and silencing my most powerful weapon, my voice. That voice might speak through a vote, a prayer, an essay or e-mail, a contribution, or a picket line. I now watch the scrolling list of fallen soldiers each week, forcing myself to read each name. By the end, I am crying. Tears indicate that my heart is open. Who would I be as a writer without an open heart? Not much of a writer at all, comes the answer, and not much of a person either.

When we learn the Wisdom of Fierce Compassion, we develop awareness of choices and the willingness to discover the pattern of our inner lives as separate from the patterns of our outer culture. As women manifest fierce compassion as part of conscious femininity, they integrate their masculine side. They also empower men to manifest conscious masculinity and to integrate their feminine side. Through fierce compassion, Lord Mother calls us to live our lives meaningfully in a way that does the least harm to others and to the earth.

The Wisdom of Diversity

The fourth wisdom honors differences and the synthesis of wholeness. Synthesis allows us to see the bigger picture, bringing together various pieces without obscuring or erasing the qualities of the individual parts. The Wisdom of Diversity teaches that every form holds its own blessing. Difference is life; without diversity there is no existence. Diversity is at the center of creativity. Millions of ways exist to express the same thing. The artist's role is to find a fresh and new way to awaken the human spirit.

The Wisdom of Diversity teaches us to honor our voice by letting go of comparison. Each voice is unique and, like a bell, has its own peal. This wisdom teaches us to respect opinions different from our own. We can like or dislike another writer's style or her choice of content while we praise her willingness to write what is true for her. Our preferences do not make us or anyone else right or wrong.

By exploring the Wisdom of Diversity, we learn that there is space for many voices, points of view, kinds

In the spirit of not knowing, women of different ethnic and cultural backgrounds could greet one another with fierce compassion and examine their shared ecosystem as women.

of writing, and content. Not everyone will like the way we write or what we have to say, and that is a wonderful thing. There is room for us. Just as we resonate with certain authors, certain readers will resonate with us.

Many women want to reach across racial, economic, and cultural divides, knowing that commonalities among women outnumber differences. Years ago, the leader of an African American ministry told me that if black women and white women could ever sit down together for a true dialogue, many of America's social and racial problems could be solved. She and I agreed that if women of different races could sit in a circle to write together, this dialogue might be possible. In the spirit of not knowing, women of different ethnic and cultural backgrounds could greet one another with fierce compassion and examine their shared ecosystem as women. From this encounter, groups would learn synthesis: how the qualities present in diversity contribute to a powerful, effective, and miraculous whole.

As women and as writers, we can learn to synthesize our masculine and feminine energies. We learn to fully accept and honor the feminine and its rhythms. We find our own relationship with our writing and our own cycles for creating. We willingly go into the darkness and mystery of the archetypal womb to face ourselves. This exploration heightens our awareness of the roles the feminine and masculine play in our individual psyches and learning styles because of biologic, familial, and cultural patterns.

As we search ourselves, we invite our positive masculine attributes to assist us so that we can finally synthesize the many ways they can support and lead us. As I discovered in writing this book, the masculine allows us to analyze, plan, and set objectives. We need these skills, and we need to know when to use them. Many of us flounder, however, if we try to create by using these skills in the early stages of writing a book, story, or article.

As stated earlier, I attempted to begin this book by creating an outline, a linear approach that has served me well with nonfiction in the past. The book shunned this approach because it denied the very feminine creative process about which I wrote. The directive model instructs us to assess the goal and then build the path to achieve it, usually through an outline. This method conflicts with the feminine's intuitive approach, to begin with inner knowing and discover where it leads step-by-step. Having been trained in the directive-linear model, we often feel a need to learn the rules and techniques of writing without first enriching the soil through process and play.

The directive-linear model has led to a proliferation of how-to-write books, which seem to be written mainly by men. The authors lay out directives like paving stones—write every day for three hours, produce a predetermined number of words or pages daily, and so on—asserting that those who follow the directions will reach the magic city of PUBLISHED BOOK.

I and other women writers rebel under such authoritarian hubris. The true issue is that the directives do not work, at least not for many women. In attempting to follow them, we lose our creative energy, the emotional connection to our work, and the belief in the authority of our own voice. Conversely, books on writing process written by women such as Annie Dillard, Natalie Goldberg, Gail Sher, and Brenda Ueland, offer me the support, inspiration, and guidance that I need.

From synthesis of the feminine with the positive masculine we receive the gifts of discernment for making wise choices, direction for maintaining focus and goals, and action for manifesting our dreams.

The message that publication confirms the value of a written work as art is untrue and does great damage to women writers, leading them to the conclusion that if they are not published, they are not writers. A friend wrote to say she had finished her third novel. Although each book has won important contests and gained the attention of agents, not one is yet published. I have no doubt that she *is* a writer and a good one. Publication will be a reward for her art, but certainly does not prove her work *as* art.

From synthesis of the feminine with the positive masculine we receive the gifts of discernment for making wise choices, direction for maintaining focus and goals, and action for manifesting our dreams. The positive masculine supports, encourages, and in-spirits us. From him, we learn the skills we eventually need to craft and refine our work: critical thinking, organization, grammar, logic, and more. The positive masculine can support us in our interactions with agents and publishers. He steadies us whenever we venture into the world of the Power Principle by reminding us of our *true power* and our true identity.

The Wisdom of Diversity calls us to meet at the center where spirit and matter, masculine and feminine, humanness and sacredness live together. From this place we share our wonder and delight; we also share our grief and our suffering. Through this sharing we unite.

Quaternity

The Wisdom of Not Knowing, the Wisdom of the Ecology of Body and Earth, the Wisdom of Fierce Compassion, and the Wisdom of Diversity form a circular quaternity. Wherever we begin, we circle down in a spiral, ever deepening into ourselves. Women's wisdom and stories have been germinating in this vortex for generations. Now is the time for them to emerge in form as writing, visual art, dance, and leadership. Now is the time for our wisdom and stories to *become* matter because they *do* matter. Now is the time to use our inner power, which we have beyond measure, to create the future we want to see.

Who invented lace? I see a woman look up from her spinning. Her gaze wanders from the spider web in the eaves to the skeletons of leaves left by ravenous insects and on to the fishnets drying on the wall. Hmmm, she muses, and her mind skitters like the spider itself. She connects the slender threads into a thing of beauty that will captivate the soul.

FIVE

The Blood-Raw Savage

Attending to our dark emotions is not just noticing
a feeling and then distancing ourselves from it. It's about
being mindful of emotions as bodily sensations and
experiencing them fully. ... this is a body-friendly process—
getting into the body, not away from it into our thoughts.
At the least, it's a process of becoming aware of how our
thoughts both trigger emotions and take us away from
them. Similarly, surrender is not about letting go but
about letting be. When you are open to your heart's
pain and to your body's experience of it, emotions flow in
the direction of greater healing, balance and harmony.

— Miriam Greenspan

Blood-raw savage is how I feel sometimes when the whole confabulation of the modern world overwhelms me. Every step I take requires three more, every phone call spawns five, and every e-mail another ten. The blood-raw savage comes out in me and perhaps isn't bad; stripped clean of skin, down to blood and sinew and bone, I have no purpose but to be, no code or appearance to live up to.

Instead I can relax in my chair, a chaise longue at that, and write poetry in my head. I need not even type it up and certainly not write a query and send it off with an self-addressed stamped envelope.

No, this blood-raw savage shuns the modern way and walks through woods, stares down the rude people at the market, and gladly swipes the plate of food sitting on the pickup counter at the trattoria.

No one says a word to the blood-raw savage, having never seen such a being so daring, so brazen, so bloody, so free.

i. Minding the Body

The blood-raw savage is the heart of my creativity, which can only *be* creative if brazen and raw and free. The blood-raw savage leaves the tribe in order to thrive. To be creative, to be a writer, requires questioning, and at times rejecting, the societal collective. Creativity is necessarily unconventional and can only be inspired outside the usual social boundaries. We women are challenged by this demand. Through generations we have integrated messages of our intellectual inferiority and of the limitations imposed by our role as nurturers. Our very bodies seem to conspire against our desire to express our innermost selves. Our biological function is to create and raise children. Though hopefully we respect and honor this role, many of us feel pulled between—sometimes pulled apart by—our love for our families and our need for creative expression and inner fulfillment.

Freeing the Body

The blood-raw savage is what our writing leads us toward: the embodiment of our unique perspective and therefore of our creative potential. Full embodiment of our individuality and our creativity requires us to reencounter all our history—all our experience, feelings, and emotions—

Whenever we release our inhibitions and relax into our bodies, messages from the unconscious arise spontaneously from the body and become conscious in the brain.

many of which we have only partially lived. To embody our lives, we must tap into the unconscious where all of our experience is stored and permit what is there to become conscious. This movement from unconscious to conscious results spontaneously from creative expression, meditation, and bodywork. In fact, if we attempt to make it happen we are likely to block the flow through endless self-analysis or denial and avoidance. Whenever we release our inhibitions and relax into our bodies, messages from the unconscious arise spontaneously from the body and become conscious in the brain.

Dreams provide entrance into the world of unlimited creativity. We enter through a relaxed state into a symbolic world of imagination. When we attend to dreams by writing them down and listening to their messages, they enrich and transform our lives, as well as inform our creativity. Although we sometimes treat our dream messages as miracles or voices from the Great Beyond, I am convinced that most dreams tell us what we already know and are unable or unwilling to consciously acknowledge.

I once misplaced a strand of pearls. I had inherited the necklace and its value was beyond monetary. After much frantic searching, certain I had inadvertently thrown the necklace away, I asked for a dream to tell me where it was. I wrote down my question three times and repeated *I will remember my dreams* as I fell asleep. The resulting dream led me to my lingerie drawer, which I had turned out and pawed through at least twice. The pearls were there, tucked neatly into an old tennis sock for safekeeping.

Thomas Edison took frequent naps, resting in his chair several times a day. If he had a problem with an invention, he would hold a ball bearing in his hand and focus on the issue as he fell asleep. As he relaxed into sleep he dropped all conscious effort. This spaciousness allowed the information he already had about the problem to rearrange into a new pattern. When the ball bearing fell to the floor, he awoke with fresh insight that led him closer to his goal.

We tend to treat the inspiration that comes while standing in the shower, on our knees weeding the garden, or waiting for the stop light to change as divinely guided because it seemingly appears from nowhere in a form we believe we could not have conceived if we "tried." While it is true that exerting effort blocks the creative flow, those answers and inspirations, the visions and knowing already exist within our cells. Divine inspiration? Yes, we can say so if we believe we contain a divine spark, a soul, a connection with something greater within us. What we should *not* do is assume that only some people have access to such inspiration. Access is granted to she who waits and listens and attends. We can find our own examples merely by thumbing through old journals of freewriting in which the occasional image is so rich we question if we wrote it. I have begun putting my initials in the margins beside such gems so I will not mistake them for quotations I copied from others.

Our uniqueness as humans and as writers is found in the body, the receptacle of all we have experienced through the senses. Recent research in neurophysiology and molecular biology shows that our emotional and feeling states are generated by our cells and not, as was once thought, by the brain. Receptor cells throughout the body receive the information, transmitting it to the limbic brain, that part of our brain unique to mammals that gives us emotions and the instinct to suckle and care for our young. The limbic brain developed long before the neocortex gave us the ability to reason, plan, think abstractly, or talk. In fact, our emotional experience has little or nothing to do with our ability to reason. Our emotions precede our thoughts. We only become conscious of emotions when the limbic brain transfers the information to the neocortex. At that point, we form ideas and concepts about what we are feeling.

To write honestly requires the writer to engage her emotions before she seeks the words to contain and translate them to the reader. One reason a reader may not respond to a particular book is because the author's writing style does not resonate with the reader's emotional experience. As a result, the reader's rational mind rejects—or at least does not embrace—the author's work. This emotional preferencing guides our friendships, marriages, and choice of everything from art to cars. Knowing this helps us remain more detached when we are faced with rejection letters or bad reviews. Not everyone will like what we write. All we can do is write honestly from our own emotional reservoir. Our words will find those readers who resonate with them.

The Body Is the Unconscious Mind

Our mind can be defined as the unceasing flow of information among the body's cells, according to Dr. Candace Pert, biophysicist and author of *Molecules of Emotion: The Science behind Mind-Body Medicine*. Interestingly, the concept of equating, rather than differentiating, the body and the mind is also found in ancient Tibetan Buddhist texts. Dr. Reginald Ray, Buddhist scholar and author of *Touching Enlightenment: Finding Realization in the Body*, says the body is the subconscious mind, the same subconscious—or unconscious—mind defined by Sigmund Freud.

Results indicate that when people write about traumatic events and the emotions those events arouse, they experience long-term health benefits even though they initially feel disturbed by the writing.

Studies of the bodymind by Pert and others contribute to the science of psycho-immunology that examines how thoughts and emotions affect our immune systems. Pert asserts that the immune system mimics our states of mind and that this information is communicated through the body by our emotions. In *Opening Up: The Healing Power of Expressing Emotions*, psychologist James W. Pennebaker presents his own and others' research on writing and immune function. Results indicate that when people write about traumatic events *and* the emotions those events arouse, they experience long-term health benefits even though they initially feel disturbed by the writing. The physical and emotional health of this group improves significantly more than that of a group that writes only about the traumatic events or that only vents their feelings.

Pennebaker believes the translation of emotions into language creates the health benefit. Through language, we organize our experiences into coherent stories, giving them form and making them easier to deal with. Writing makes the incomprehensible meaningful, moves us toward understanding and resolution, and in the process releases stored emotions and promotes healing in the bodymind. Talking about our trauma also helps,

Rather than viewing the natural rhythms of our bodies as imposing limitations, we can see them as guides for inner understanding and creative development.

but talking requires a skilled and receptive listener. Writing allows us to tell the story honestly without interruption, explanation, or consideration for anyone else. To impact the immune system, it does not matter whether anyone hears or reads the story, what the event was, or how long ago it occurred.

The seemingly miraculous connection between writing and the immune system results from cracking through inhibition. Simply put, keeping secrets and maintaining denial requires physical energy, energy our bodies could use in healthier ways.

We inhibit the emotional processing of both positive and negative experiences for various reasons. For example, our physical survival may depend on repressing the emotions caused by traumatic events. Whenever we are unable to comprehend an experience at the moment of occurrence, whether traumatic or not, we repress the memory and its emotions. As children, we did not cognitively understand many of our experiences. Even in the course of daily life as adults, we do not stop to truly live and understand our moment-to-moment existence. As we move from activity to activity, we create distractions to avoid processing our experiences and feeling our emotions. We call this disconnect between our experiences and the unacknowledged emotions stored in our bodies "stress."

Our bodies, as seats of the unconscious, hold all the experiences we have not thoroughly lived, and emotions and feelings we have not allowed ourselves to express, both pleasurable and painful. Glimmers of these often appear to us as "abiding images"—an image that we recognize as having emotional content although we cannot explain why. Poet Cathy Smith Bowers suggests that we keep lists of these images and explore them through our writing. Although the exact memory may never surface, the emotional experience will appear through metaphor, character, symbol, and theme. If we do not force revelation but trust the process, our body reveals its secrets at a pace that allows understanding, acceptance, and healing.

ii. Writing a Woman's Body

As women, our bodies hold generations of shame, blame, betrayal, and victimization, both given and received. Many of our negative emotions are centered on the body itself. Even as liberated women today, we treat the cycles of the female body as disease states and accept and make jokes about premenstrual syndrome (PMS) and menopause. Instead of connecting to our body's wisdom, we deny the body's deep needs.

To practice the hard work of writing, the blood-raw savage insists we confront life raw, unearthing and releasing the stories that can heal us. In this way we claim our creativity and release our cultural conditioning. Because creative writing is somatic, grounded in sensations, sensory experience, feelings, and emotions, we can rely on the body to lead us. The exploration is not cognitive but energetic. We do not need to know the story line. We need only to give the body, with its emotions and feelings, the freedom to express.

A young artist friend tracks her creativity and emotions in relation to her ovulation. She finds her creativity surges when she is fertile, while an interval of depression and doubt accompanies her menses. She equates this latter period with an innate grief at the loss of a creative opportunity.

Very possibly, the degree to which we block access to our bodies is the degree to which our truth remains unexpressed.

Tribal cultures that honored women's rhythms understood women to hold the creative future of the culture—not only because they produced children, but because they fathomed the sacred nature of the cycles of creation. Women in these cultures celebrated their creative and intuitive potential by withdrawing as a group from their village every month. Another reason existed for the women's isolation during their menses: their ability to bleed but not die from their bleeding was interpreted as a supernatural power to defy death. Undoubtedly, the men felt safer when menstruating females practiced their magic outside the daily life of the village.

By attending to our physical rhythms, we modern women can find our way to becoming more accepting and nurturing of ourselves. Rather than viewing the natural rhythms of our bodies as imposing limitations, we can see them as guides for inner understanding and creative development.

The blood-raw savage has an ally in menopause, a time at which, according to gynecologist Dr. Christiane Northrup, the shift in hormonal balance frees us to focus on our soul's demands instead of on society's. Many of us at this stage of life discover we are less afraid to speak out and are more willing to use our increased intuitive ability and wisdom and to explore our creativity.

Listening to the body is not easy for most of us because we have long-established patterns of ignoring and neglecting it. We also fear the call of the blood-raw savage because she lures us out of our comfort zones. Yet, our bodies are the source of our voice—and more than anything, we long for our voice to be heard. We must acknowledge the ways in which our culture, families, and we, ourselves, have metaphorically cut our throats and forced us to swallow our words and our truth. Such acknowledgement arouses anger, judgment, and a myriad of other negative emotions that we have learned are unacceptable for women to express. The blood-raw savage urges us to take the step. As creatives we must learn to thoroughly live the present moment, as well as experience and express what the body has stored. Very possibly, the degree to which we block access to our bodies is the degree to which our truth remains unexpressed.

Writing Raw

To walk around raw, confronting life as writers without averting our gaze from our own or others' suffering, is hard work. While the pen empties out much of what we see, we learn through writing to experience life deeply. In *The Creating Brain*, Nancy Anderson surveys studies of creativity and mental illness. She reports that not only is mental illness more prevalent in literary writers, but that depression, especially bipolar disorder, is the most common disorder. The supposition is that wide mood swings may actually contribute to the creative depth and breadth of a writer's work. Virginia Woolf, who recognized the positive impact of her bouts of "madness" on her writing, might agree.

My husband spent most of his career in sales, which he describes as allowing him to be "manic-depressive with just cause." Creatives could describe themselves the same way. Every serious artist and writer I have known experiences mood swings, though few are diagnosed with a disorder. Perhaps, as Anderson suggests, wide mood swings contribute to creative depth, but they might also result from combining the empathy aroused by a deep engagement in life with the emotional turmoil of the creative effort. We get stuck and experience despair; the writing flows and we rejoice. We finish the manuscript filled with possibility and confidence only to fall into postpartum depression. Back and forth we swing between absolute belief in ourselves and absolute belief that no one will read, enjoy, or understand our work. To survive, we embrace the swings as part of the process and accept the necessity to keep writing. Moods, after all, are simply emotions that ebb and flow. Chanting "this too shall pass" may be the most helpful remedy.

At the same time that mood swings accompany many serious writers, writing can also relieve depression. In my classes, I watch women who arrive visibly depressed create new lives. Over time, the effect is dramatic: the victim disappears and

Within the spaciousness of the belly is truly where the Muse resides, not hanging around the rafters or perched on our shoulder whispering in our ear.

a confident decision-maker emerges; playful and fanciful poetry and prose replace controlled storytelling. As Eve Ensler, author of *The Vagina Monologues*, says, "If you just tell the truth, things change." Things change on the molecular level and that changes everything.

Our culture is obsessed with the body to the point of objectifying it. This objectification leads to alienation that in turn contributes to eating disorders, addictions, debilitating self-esteem issues, and suicide. Writers and other artists, along with practitioners of many Eastern religions, maintain a higher degree of physical awareness because art—spiritual, written, visual—arises from our inner relationship to the outer world through the body.

In the West, we speak of the mind/body/spirit connection as if these were three separate modes; in actuality no separation exists among them. Separating the body, the domain of the feminine, from mind or spirit is another way in which we disengage and denigrate the feminine by giving ascendancy to the masculine domains of intellect and spirit. The new discoveries of science will eventually enter cultural awareness and shift this long-held belief in the mind/body/spirit split.

Soft Belly

"Soft belly," I tell my students. "Before writing, be quiet. Come into your body, bringing your awareness to your belly, the center of the creative impulse." Within the spaciousness of the belly is truly where the Muse resides, not hanging around the rafters or perched on our shoulder whispering in our ear. The more we bring our awareness to this place, the more we notice the tension there and elsewhere in the body. When we practice this, "soft belly" becomes a bell calling us home.

I practiced sitting meditation many years on my own before learning that the very posture in which a meditator sits *is* meditation. Once I received instruction on correct posture, my experience shifted. Without correct posture of the body, the mind remains chaotic.

Sitting practice has taught me to stay with the emotion that arises, no matter how painful. Culturally we are taught not only to avoid painful feelings, but that there is something wrong with us for experiencing them. The best example is the American attitude toward grief which can be summed up by "get over it and soon!" We are generally intolerant of negative or painful emotions, our own or others', and therefore overlook and devalue what they can teach us about ourselves and our connection with others. The ability to deal with our emotions and feelings by staying with our experience of them in our bodies strengthens us creatively.

Staying with the emotion is necessary for a writer. Readers recognize pretense and denial. As writers, if we pay attention to our bodies they tell us when we are running away. The scenes that are the hardest to write are those that cause us to face our own demons. Likewise, we find it difficult to write honestly, but without overwhelming pathos, of a traumatic event in our own lives. Before we have had time to process and learn and heal from an event, our writing is likely to be pure catharsis—helpful for ourselves, but not necessarily beneficial to a reader.

Staying with the emotion, no matter when it slams me, requires my willingness to feel and explore it in my body. During a massage, the therapist asked how I felt.

"Sad."

"How do you know?"

The question startled me. How did I know? I had never considered how I identified an emotion. I had to scan my body to discover sensations that would give me the answer.

My words came out haltingly: A tightness in my throat. My heart feels slightly closed. My mouth seems dry and my shoulders a little tense.

That is how I knew sad. My body told me.

Felt Sense Makes Sense

Rather than identifying the emotion and looking for its physical expression, we can turn the technique around and scan the body for a physical *felt sense.* Discussed by psychologist Eugene Gendlin in his book *Focusing,* felt sense is the body's ability to talk to us without words. We begin at the soles of the feet and proceed up the legs to the perineum, the area between the external genitalia and the anus. We pay particular attention to the space in the lower belly, then move to the chest behind the bottom ribs, the space beneath the collarbones including the upper back and shoulders, and the throat, arms, hands, and head.

Symbolically, the perineum relates to entry and to connection with the earth, the lower belly with creativity, the solar plexus with intuition, the chest with compassion, the throat with communication, the center of the forehead (third eye) with insight and intuition, and the crown (above the head) with release and connection with the soul.

After scanning the whole body, we allow our attention to find the felt sense, a spot in the body that seems to call for exploration. By focusing on this spot, we can detect its nature—density, temperature, size, texture. Sometimes a picture or word will spontaneously arise in relation to the sensation, but conceptualizing is not the intent. Instead, we simply stay aware of the present experience and allow insight to arise. This quiet attention is freeing—it allows us to let go of our own story line, that repetitive tape in our heads that usually revolves around judgment and shame and victimization. As writers, this is how we find the distance to tell our own stories and how we can use our own experience as jumping-off places into fictional lives.

Gendlin also suggests that, when discussing or thinking about an issue or problem, it is helpful to drop into the body for this felt sense instead of trying to "figure it out" in our heads. Through very gentle exploration, the body will reveal the answer or a direction toward the answer.

iii. The Arc of Writing

While working on this word circle, an insight arose related to a question I have long pondered: exactly what we do refer to when we say "writing"? Journalists, technical writers, copywriters, novelists, and poets can equally claim, "I am a writer."

I envisioned an arc illustrating a continuum of writing. The left side of the continuum contains factual writing, beginning with technical writing—directions for taking prescriptions, programming the VCR, and the like—and passing through research writing, dissertations, and journalism to opinion, personal essay, letters, and personal journal writing. From memoir and creative nonfiction, we drift down the right hand side of the arc; we move from fictionalized memoir through genre fiction to literary fiction, from the concrete and realistic to the imaginary, symbolic, and metaphorical, and finally to poetry with its own gradations of complexity and experimentation. The continuum ends in avant-garde and experimental poetry. Avant-garde

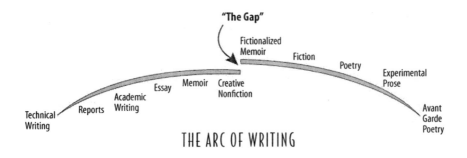

THE ARC OF WRITING

poets reject the mainstream and play the edge of language, form, and style; they serve as messengers, foretelling their culture's direction.

As a continuum, the arc does not present one placement as better than another. It is not meant to suggest that avant garde poetry is an art to which writers should aspire, or that writing magazine articles instead of literary fiction is a less worthy undertaking. The placements are mine and are subjective. The journey we take and where we encounter the gap differ for each of us. The purpose of the continuum is to encourage understanding of what is involved in traversing the gap— to examine what within us must shift.

The gap represents the emotional risk we take when we choose to leave the familiar and commit to a life of perpetual discovery. For me, this gap was the transition from fact-based to creative writing. This shift involves shifting from cognition to physical and emotional perception, intellect to body, telling to showing, and from writing *about* our experience to writing *from* our experience. Before I could traverse my own gap, I had to move from "I want to write" to "I can write." Once across the chasm, I could finally say with conviction, "I am a writer." I could embrace my joy in writing with a diminished need for explanation, justification, or approval.

I think back through the many women who have come to my classes; some stayed for years, others left as soon as they could. Of those who stayed, some struggled until I almost gave up hope of their progress. Others, shown a path, flew along it. I have observed these differences, and looking at this continuum arc, I get an inkling of why.

Women who enjoy writing have good language-arts skills. I was one of these, competent in the school-related writing represented on the left side of the arc—essay, grammar, punctuation, structure. I could write press releases, marketing materials, and newspaper and magazine articles with ease.

To make the shift to creative writing, I had to choose to leave the comfort of competence. For years I sought someone to tell me how to write from my imagination, to give me an instruction book like *The Little, Brown Handbook* that enumerates the rules of grammar with clear examples. I recognize now that the women who quickly depart from my classes are those seeking such a book. As soon as they realize I will not provide it, they flee.

For myself, I had to release the hope that someone would save me from what I understood to be an arduous and painful journey. Fortunately, I never had a teacher willing to take the power I would readily have given away. I had no opportunity to cling or fixate on a person or approach. I simply had to trudge through, step-by-step. I recognize now that the women I watch struggling are simply trudging. As long as I can see the struggle, they *are* making progress. I have learned to trust that one day these women will sit down and make the leap across the chasm they have been scouting.

When we insist on seeking an intellectual understanding to a problem rather than listening to the body's intelligence, we experience creative aridity or a complete block of the creative process.

Our educational system trains us primarily on the left side of the continuum as we learn to write essays and research papers. The transition to creative writing can be particularly difficult for those of us who feel our creative selves have been stifled, especially if our writing has been limited to and prescribed by academia, marketing, science, or research. Adept at using language to explain, organize, persuade, and direct, we are challenged when asked to use words to communicate and evoke emotions and feelings through sensory descriptions, imaginary characters, and exploration of conflict.

We experience a steep learning curve as we confront the shift out of our heads and into our bellies and emotions. The right side of the arc of writing requires that we loosen up by letting go of the writing we have done in school or at work. We do not throw away skills of orga-nization, grammar, and linear structure, but initially we play without them so we can learn how to risk writing freely.

We can get stuck and resist crossing the gap. Becoming mired in our own angst in personal journaling is a frequent cause of stuck-ness. Compulsive churning and figuring out actually separates us from our bodies by keeping us in our heads. The creative process is a visceral one more than it is mental. When we insist on seeking an intellectual under-standing to a problem rather than listening to the body's intelligence, we experience creative aridity or a complete block of the creative process.

The arc of writing helps me visualize what may happen in my class-es as a woman experiences the freedom of dropping into her writing. Over time, she will move from personal stories to fiction or poetry. She may move back again into memoir or creative nonfiction, taking the elements of fiction and poetry with her. The writing becomes deeper, freer, and more identifiably hers. She finds her voice. This discovery translates into her life as self-assuredness, strength, and the courage to risk being who she is.

Fierce compassion for herself and the human condition drives the blood-raw savage forward. Women know how to birth possibility. We carry the knowledge and strength of the "how" in our bodies once we learn to open ourselves to our feminine nature. We must become the blood-raw savage and dare to allow ourselves to be gripped hard by our stories, to let them wrangle us to the ground, until we find ourselves dancing and shar-ing them with others.

The blood-raw savage stands solidly on the earth, her Mother. She relies on this base for comfort and sustenance; she is not afraid of the Mother's darkness or of her crystal caves. The blood-raw savage is the one in each of us who stands up to name what others do not want to see. The world needs women's truth and, in order to survive physically and soul-fully, we need to speak it. When we begin to write, we do not know what that truth is. We may not find out until we are finished, and sometimes not even then. When we let the blood-raw savage write, the body tells the tale, and we cannot help but write toward the truth.

SIX

Risking Words

The trouble is, if you don't risk anything, you risk even more.

— Erica Jong

Meaning, if it existed at all, was unstable and could not survive the slightest reshuffling of letters. One gust of wind and Santa became Satan. A slip of the pen and pears turned into pearls.

— Lorrie Moore

Words.
Words curled around
me, led me dancing
through green meadows,
sang praise, sent the bullfrog
from his rock into cool depths.
Marching letters slouched, slinked, and staggered,
left sidewalks sprouting wildflowers of meaning.

My child-time words took a sideways run toward freedom—
sheep became scheep, my ships schips.
"I'm not tongue tied, I just don't talk plain," I explained,
remaining deaf to my aberration.
At 22 I entered a graduate school in speech therapy—ignorant,
never having received this help myself.
Heal yourself first. The famous professor frowned
behind his words as their deepest truth eluded
both of us in the smoke from his pipe.

I banished the aberration,
talked plain. Still only pen
on paper untied the tongue
that could not speak aloud
to an audience that would not listen.
Danger lay in loosing words, so words took root in me.
My friends the words wriggled out on blue-lined paper.

Wispy whispering words ploughed ground
for cast-off seeds.

i. Defying the Emperor

Two thousand years ago, women in the remote Jiangyong County of China created Nushu, a secret language, to share their feelings with one another. Although the emperor of the time had decreed that the penalty for creating new languages was death for oneself, one's family, and nine related families, the women took the risk. They did what they needed to do to survive in the near-prisons of their homes. They spoke and sang Nushu when they gathered to do handwork and when cloistered together before wedding celebrations. They shared the secrets of their hearts in poems and letters only other women could read. At the turn of the millennium, three women remained living who could speak of how Nushu allowed them to overcome their loneliness and isolation and enjoy a small rebellion against the oppression that confined them.

Language is an attribute of the masculine principle. The masculine holds the rational, linear, and analytic, while the feminine holds synthesis along with the intuitive and circuitous, the stuff that stories are made of. Read the sentence again and you understand the weight of words. The words representing the feminine have a derogatory tone— changing, deviating, indirect, interrupted, roundabout. Ah, these silly women with their intuitions and their indirect and circuitous thinking! Yes, and is it not exactly this kind of thinking that is needed to be a writer or artist? Is it not this kind of thinking that sees possibilities, makes connections between disparate ideas, and leaps where the rational mind fears to go?

The time may have come again for women to risk creating a new language, or to use language in new ways in order to more truly express the feminine way of seeing the world. The more often we risk telling our stories in our own manner and style, the more we will influence the prevailing worldview, and the more power we will exert in the world. The Power Principle, however, has controlled most of the pub-

Dreams, being circuitous adventures into creative fantasy, are neither linear nor rational. Their meaning lies in symbolism and metaphor particular to the individual dreamer, while also leaping into the archetypal world that crosses time and culture.

lishing world for centuries. To the degree the Power Principle prevails, the language of books, as well as their content, will be subject to its standards.

A shift is occurring now as more women write and seek ways to be heard. Some are publishing as cooperative teams like Tres Chicas in Taos, New Mexico, and Wild Girl Publishing in Santa Cruz, California, so as to be independent of corporations. Other feminist and women-led presses exist to support women's writing efforts. Like the women who created Nushu under the noses of their husbands and the emperor, women today know how to exert power and influence by following the wall as far as necessary to discover a gate.

Initially, women must dare to speak a language that reaches other women through the universality of women's experience. A friend who traveled to the former Soviet Union with one of the first citizen exchanges said, "It was easy for me to relate to the women. We took out the photos of our families. One woman showed me a picture of her son in his military uniform, pantomimed a gun, then pointed to her own eyes and ran her fingers down her cheeks like tears. I nodded, touched my heart, and gestured from it to her. We both understood perfectly."

Poetry, song, and story serve a woman's creative spirit and style because they employ metaphor and create space for engendering both mystical and emotional experience. A fellow writer, attempting to write about a profound personal and spiritual experience, became discouraged when the structure and form of language deprived her experience of depth and impact. Finally she sat in meditation and wrote whatever arose. The result came in fragments, single words, and disjointed images.

Our feminine nature thrives on metaphor and paradox and tolerates spaciousness around concepts and ideas.

This writer also teaches women to use dreams to access their spiritual centers. The language she used to describe her experience was not unlike that of dreams. Dreams may provide the key to the new feminine language. Dreams, being circuitous adventures into creative fantasy, are neither linear nor rational. Their meaning lies in symbolism and metaphor particular to the individual dreamer while also leaping into the archetypal world that crosses time and culture.

"Perhaps what you've written is poetry," I said.

I could hear her smile across the phone line. "Perhaps so. Perhaps so."

To English speakers, at least, poetry accepts and rewards these original utterances better than prose. "The activity of poetry is to tell us we must change our lives," writes poet Jane Hirschfield. She explains that poetry does this by repeatedly asking questions that can only be answered with our whole beings. We can use Centered Writing Practice to wake ourselves up to our souls in a similar way, slipping into the unconscious to reclaim the parts buried there. By engaging process through Centered Writing Practice, we often find new language emerging in fresh images and "errors" in spelling, grammar, and word choice that capture our intent better than standard English. Sometimes a character's voice arises to tell a story we have never heard.

Women creatives revel in this type of exploration. Our feminine nature thrives on metaphor and paradox and tolerates spaciousness around concepts and ideas. The sacred poetry of Izumi Shikibu (eleventh century, Japan), Mechthild of Magdeburg (thirteenth century, Germany), Bibi Hayati (nineteenth century, Persia), and Gabriela Mistral (twentieth century, Chile) exemplifies this spaciousness in the language of the feminine. I am touched deeply by the words of these poets. I cannot explain the feelings they evoke or their meaning; any effort to do so diminishes the impact. I experience the meaning within my body because the words capture something understood by my soul rather than my mind.

ii. Word-View, Worldview

Our language and view of the world are intertwined. The English language was exported to Asian and African countries during the expansion of the British Empire in the nineteenth century. After World War II, the rise of the United States as a world political and economic power resulted in English becoming the preferred second language around the world. An unintended consequence of the widespread use of English is the absorption by other cultures of the American worldview, including the imbalanced and negative masculine of the Power Principle.

When I studied language in graduate school, I developed a fascination for its aliveness, how language evolves over time to meet the needs of its culture, how children acquire and are culturally shaped by it, and how the loss of language by an individual or a tribe isolates and devastates. Language allows us to categorize and therefore to associate seemingly disparate objects and ideas. It also, however, restricts our thoughts by the type of categories it creates, the number of different words applied to a phenomena (such as snow or clouds or sadness or love), and by the constraints of the grammatical structure.

Languages differ in their complexity and levels of meaning. I have read that sacred writing has seven levels of meaning that a reader accesses as she or he progresses in spiritual understanding. Ancient sacred texts read in the Western world are necessarily translations from Latin, ancient Greek, Sanskrit, ancient Arabic, and other languages no longer spoken. All translations are dependent on the translator's knowledge of the original language and the cultural context in which it was used, as well as the translator's alignment with the "heart" of the author. As readers, we interpret through our own understanding, thus adding our own layer of "translation."

I am curious about ideographic languages like Chinese in which a single character can hold many, and often opposing, meanings so that the symbol itself is a metaphor. Additionally, Chinese is tonal, adding a dimension that English speakers find hard to imagine. Are Chinese and other ideographic and tonal languages more feminine? I wonder.

In English the subject comes first, implying the importance of the actor over the acted upon. In other languages, the subject holds a more subordinate place in the sentence. There may be languages in which there is no subject, where action arises independent of an actor. In English, we delineate gender through pronouns—he and she. In Latinate languages like French and Spanish, and in German as well, all nouns have gender designations of masculine, feminine, or neuter. In contrast, Cherokee pronouns are neutral and do not designate gender. Possibly, this is a reflection of the matriarchal culture.

Time is also handled differently in different languages and is generally reflected in cultural attitudes. English verb forms delineate past, present, and future. Culturally, Americans are very time conscious and treat time as a tangible object like money or bananas. We commonly say we can save time, spend time, waste time, use time, and run out of time. Other languages show time only by referring to natural events such as moon phases or seasons. In these cultures, time is cyclical and eternal. Time cannot be spent, wasted, used, or saved; one can never run out of time even at death.

Story, dreams, and poetry—all metaphor—are the language of the feminine. Each relies on the relationship between the teller or unconscious mind and the listener or conscious mind.

In Native American cultures, things work on "Indian time." Non-natives sometimes use these words with disparagement because things are late by non-native standards. Culturally, however, Indian time supports the understanding that things occur when the time is right. If we are at one with the world, everything will occur in its own time. This attitude and the language used to express it are attuned to the cyclical, earth-driven rhythm of the feminine.

The languages of tribal cultures are often very concrete and deal with day-to-day experiences. Abstractions and ideas are relayed through metaphor, ritual, dreams, and story—people intuit the meaning of the story or ritual and apply it to their lives. From *Aesop's Fables* to *The Tales of Peter Rabbit* and *The Adventures of Alice in Wonderland*, story captures the universality of the human experience.

Story, dreams, and poetry—all metaphor—are the language of

Silence and solitude provide food for the writer that is as essential as observing and interacting with the world.

the feminine. Each relies on the relationship between the teller or unconscious mind and the listener or conscious mind. The teller trusts the listener to enter into the story and understand what is not spoken. The teller accepts that each listener will hear the story from her own perspective and experience and therefore no two will hear it exactly the same. This is quite a different approach from laying out rational argument with the intent of persuasion. Like the storytellers throughout time, women can awaken people to themselves by becoming more conscious of language as a tool for reshaping the world. As we explore the use of language in fresh and innovative ways, new words, structures, and images will emerge that match our experience as women.

iii. Creating Silent Space

The language of the feminine embraces silence. Silence creates rhythm and builds tension. Silence provides the spaciousness through which the sacred speaks.

In mainstream American culture, silence is a vacuum to be filled; it makes us uncomfortable and can denote disapproval or withdrawal. We now walk around connected to conversations and music through cell phones and iPods so that we block out even the sounds of nature.

While working with the Eastern Band of Cherokee Indians, I learned silence can be as communicative as intonation or gesture. Even though most members of the Eastern Band speak English and do not know their native tongue, silence is still used as the container for discussion. When an important decision is considered in a group, members listen to the facts and then sit in silence. Periodically, someone will make a comment or ask a question, but there is little discussion as experienced in a non-native meeting. Finally, the leader will ask for a vote. In the silence, each person has made up his or her mind independent of the influence of others. As a non-native participant, I had to learn to hold the silence and allow it to do its work.

Silence and solitude provide food for the writer that is as essential as observing and interacting with the world. Whether a woman accepts or rejects this confinement, she may struggle with aspects of her feminine nature. A woman thrives on relationship, but writing requires closing doors, at least temporarily. At a certain point in the process of writing this book, I became a bad neighbor and churlish friend. Too much social interaction drained my energy. I said no to everything and everyone I could. I risked friendships and family relationships.

Women's receptivity can encourage a kind of inertia, so once I close the door to write, I feel that I am running toward and pulling away at the same time. I must work at discerning the difference between receptivity and procrastination, and between processing and producing. At times, the hardest thing I can do is stay in the chair, especially when I perceive someone needs me. At those times my writing seems utterly selfish. I must remind myself that I am in a birth process, incarnating words. I cannot stop the labor pains to do the laundry or attend a friend's luncheon.

There is no right way to make space for the solitude and silence of writing. We have individual biorhythms contributing to our best time for focused work. We have individual lives and family demands and jobs. We may have to be content with keeping a writer's notebook until our children grow to a certain age. Instead of bemoaning this necessity, we could choose to celebrate the opportunity to befriend our observations and our words. We always have choices. Choosing consciously avoids bitterness and resentment. The edge we walk to balance our inner and outer lives so we can create is always in danger of crumbling and in need of focused attention. Balance is not static, but an individual process of continual adjustment.

Today I have taken advantage of a friend's absence to use her house as a writing retreat. Today I have only words to arrange on the page and the simultaneous urge for distraction. All day, until my husband comes by with dinner, I face myself across the white expanse of paper. I have given myself room; I have shown up. Showing up is not magic, but I believe it is enough.

A Tibetan word *re-dok* combines the word for hope and the word for fear, suggesting that we cannot have one without the other. Re-dok springs from our belief that there is an answer outside to an inner feeling of lack. As a writer I frequently visit the world of re-dok. To ease the discomfort of this feeling, I am forced to recognize that

I have to remind myself that I am not seeking perfection through my writing, I am seeking to express the imperfection that makes life rich and full of wonder.

there is something I want from the writing that is outside of myself. The answer may be simply "good writing." Yet, with this answer, I am forced to admit I want to please someone other than myself. Once I accept this, a whole troop of desires arrives—money, eminence, recognition, immortality. Re-dok is my reminder to relax and go back to writing for myself and the sake of writing.

If I cannot let go of re-dok, my husband will arrive and I will be struck with another paradox: I will feel relieved to have the distraction I longed for and depressed that I did not accomplish more with the time I had. I will feel torn between my two loves with the result that I will not be present to either and to some degree will betray each.

When the writing goes badly, nothing is wrong. Time with a blank page or a pen moving furiously across the page, time with my husband or at my desk, time walking in the woods or reading a book—all of this is writing. Writing encompasses all experiences of my life, its noise and silence, rage and peace, interaction and solitude.

My frustration with writing arises because I expect my love for it to make it easy. Yet everything I have ever learned about love tells me otherwise. The very things that cause me struggle and pain give my relationships depth. In human relationships, maturity brings an awareness of the blessings of less-than-perfection. I have to remind myself that I am not seeking perfection through my writing, I am seeking to express the imperfection that makes life rich and full of wonder.

We cannot write without risk or without self-insight or self-revelation. Yet writing is much more than emotional catharsis and cannot succeed if that is all it is. The drive to write might be viewed as an underground river of unarticulated knowledge, a felt sense that keeps surfacing, wanting definition and recognition. Our emotions and our experience rise from the body through our individual creative filters and appear in metaphors, symbols, and themes without our conscious manipulation.

Risking words risks life. My demons rage outside my door. If I ignore them, they will overwhelm me with their hammering and shouts. If I invite them in for tea and acknowledge their presence, they will eventually fall asleep on my floor. Of course, they will return each day, but over time they become tamer, more like family pets.

Only understanding and acceptance bring peace; struggle never does. This is true of nations and of individuals. Better to expend effort on no effort than to expend it on struggle. When we accept that we always stand in the midst of flux and that there is no ground to stand on that is always stable, we can expend our effort on being real and true. In this way, we learn to live with the risk of our words.

SEVEN

Be a Tree

It is not your business to determine how good it is nor how valuable nor how it compares with other expressions. It is your business to keep it yours clearly and directly, to keep the channel open. You do not even have to believe in yourself or your work. You do have to keep open and aware directly to the urges that motivate you. Keep the channel open... No artist is pleased.... [There is] no satisfaction whatever at any time... There is only a queer divine dissatisfaction, a blessed unrest that keeps us marching and makes us more alive than others.

— Martha Graham

The old tree mothers stand straight and tall, their stout waists too wide for my arms to encircle. I lay my head to a rough belly and see eye to wing, a moth dressed in brown velvet. The mother's apron smells of vanilla, and as she moves gently round her sky kitchen rearranging the clouds, she drops blossoms colored like pumpkin, spring lettuce, and crookneck squash at my feet.

"Careful," she says, as I press near. "The snail makes her slow journey, moving her house to my branches. And the ants have a home by my roots, the spiders in the shadow of my shingled bark."

I breathe in the vanilla again, pressing my ear close to her heartbeat.

"I must leave here," I say. "Give me something for remembrance."

"Be a tree," she whispers. "Be a tree."

I walk out of the forest, turning back once to see all the mothers standing there—not silent at all.

i. Self-Be

A Better Tree

For months the memory of the Great Tree Mothers dogged me, nipping at my heels and occasionally digging up and offering bones of meaning. *Be a tree. Be yourself. Sink deep, strong roots into the heart of the earth, the* mater, *the mother. Write from the heart of* mater *to discover what matters. Shrug off the anonymity long thought to be the proper condition of women, dig down deep and dare to get dirty, come up with snakes for hair like Medusa and voice the story that is yours.*

Today I sit in the garden to write, contemplating the teaching. It is a cool, overcast day in May. To sit here requires resisting the urge to weed or to transplant the painted fern being choked out by the ground cover. Around me the tree mothers dance in the afternoon breeze while a minute chartreuse spider rests on the maroon pillow in my lap. Usually I distract myself from life's circular rhythms by imposing a linear order that allows me to feel in control. I could, if I wished, become so scheduled that I would never have to consider that everything is changing and that security and knowing are illusions.

To write I become still like the seventy-foot shagbark hickory beside me. It has watched history unfold for over a hundred years and wakes each morning surprised to find my house in its yard. In the stillness I comprehend that to be a tree means to be true to my feminine nature, releasing patterns learned in order to accommodate myself to a culture that prizes (and also distorts) the masculine.

To be true to the feminine, I hear the tree mothers say, is about self-being, not self-improvement. A tree cannot be other than itself. An oak is an oak whether planted in Illinois or Arizona. The palm tree in the hotel lobby still sings songs of Jamaica as the snow piles up outside the windows in Duluth. A tree cannot become "better" at being a tree. Getting better implies something is wrong to begin with.

Many of us, on the other hand, seem intent on pruning ourselves into topiaries. We then mistake this image for our own nature, not realizing that by doing so we imprison ourselves. The degree to which a woman limits herself to preconceived roles will be reflected in her writing. Seeing this reflection can awaken her to the need for change. Then writing can provide a path for breaking the confines of the life she lives and for creating a new story for herself.

The Mandorla

Years ago I made a batik of a tree, an image of bare limbs embracing the sky above and roots embracing the earth below. Schematically, envision two circles. Below ground, one represents the feminine and process; above ground, the other represents the masculine and product.

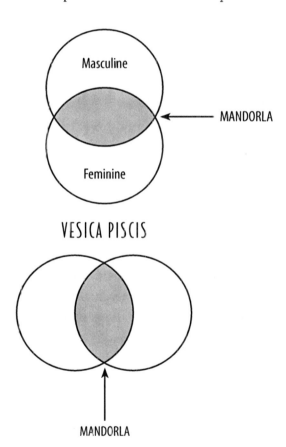

The two cannot be separated, each being necessary for the survival of the other. If a writer engages primarily in process, she will likely flounder in an emotional morass. If she approaches writing primarily from product, her writing will lack emotional depth, passion, and vibrancy.

The degree to which writing transcends the ordinary informational content of words and captures a larger truth is represented by the degree of overlap of the two circles. When the two circles overlap so that the outer edge of each circle passes through the center of the other, the symbol is called the *vesica piscis* or "bladder of the fish" and the place of overlap, the almond shape in the center, is called the *mandorla*.

When arranged horizontally, one circle beside the other, the *vesica piscis* is the ancient and universal symbol for the doorway of all life, the mandorla representing the vulva of the Great Mother. When arranged vertically, one circle above the other, the mandorla becomes the fish symbol used by Christians to identify themselves.

We experience the mandorla in that breathless moment of *One* each of us occasionally encounters, the moment we wish to freeze so that we can forever partake of its transparent sweetness. In this moment time stops, and we want to cry for the sheer beauty of it. We understand that joy is not an emotion but the physical sensation of wholeness. We know that the body is not the limit of who we are: we are light that travels great distances over billions of years through space, like water through time, and becomes in an instant, for an instant, you or me. We relive the moment when a ray of sun through the morning fog transmutes a single maple leaf to gold or when the sacred smell of silence inside an old barn speaks the stories of earth and time, of love and loss. In each of these moments, the heart splits open. We can do nothing but watch our love spill out upon the ground.

Masculine and feminine, heaven and earth, the ephemeral and the eternal meet in the mandorla, the place of oneness and nonduality. For writers, the *vesica piscis* represents the transcendence of craft—that merging of creative process with refined product that the writer reaches for. In all of these interpretations of the symbol, one thing remains clear—the circles never overlap completely. If we imagine the circles pulsating, we might get a clearer picture—one of movement flowing in and out, approach and retreat, always moving, never static.

Spiritual practitioners catch glimpses of this transcendent state and want to maintain it, thinking this is the goal of their practice. Their teachers remind them that enlightenment is not a permanent condition. In writing, it is much the same. We practice writing process in order to let go of striving for perfection and approval. Eventually we hear our voice and intuitively know when we are in the flow. We learn the elements of craft, from characterization and point of view to plotting and punctuation, as much by immersion as by direct study.

Transcendent moments occur because we practice, not as rewards or results, but simply as moments. Such moments can be touched but not held.

We strive toward the transcendence of craft where each word sparkles in its place, capturing the meaning in a translucent web. Transcendent moments occur because we practice, not as rewards or results, but simply as moments. Such moments can be touched but not held. That was Sir Lawrence Olivier's experience after a particular performance of *Hamlet:* he knew that through his craft he had excelled in a way that was both eternal and ephemeral. He did not need the applause or the reviews to tell him what had happened; he *knew*. He also knew that just as he did not intentionally make the moment occur, he could not consciously do it twice, though he might experience it again.

ii. Preparing the Ink

The Intent Is in the Line

In a class, Zen priest and calligraphy teacher Reverend Eiko Kichung Lizee talked about preparing the ink as a meditation, how she spent hours grinding the ink against the stone. She sat on the floor in her black robe to demonstrate, her tools spread before her like holy relics. Every movement was unhurried and fluid.

When it was time for the class to participate, I did not want to spend time preparing the ink. I only wanted to paint. Reflecting on my response, I understood that preparing the ink *is* the painting. Without proper ink and the one-pointed attention needed to prepare it, the image cannot emerge. The image is not an idea on paper, a pretty drawing. The image is an energetic synthesis of ink, stone, water, hand, brush, body, and the inner state of the artist. Two people can draw a circle with a broad brush and the discerning eye will know which came from the master. As Reverend Lizee told us, "You can tell the intent of the artist by the line."

The quality of our writing is best assessed, not by the seeming value of what we do, but by the inner value we place on it.

The quality of our writing is best assessed, not by the seeming value of what we do, but by the inner value we place on it. When we *do* with the awareness of *being,* the inner value is high. When value is seen only as outcome and/or money, we lose the understanding that our writing is valuable in and of itself. The product is not an object *outside* the writer, or even an extension *of* the writer; it *is* the writer. As writers we continually practice, throwing away page after page, doing revision after revision so that what eventually emerges reflects our closest approximation to the transcendence of craft that we can produce at that time.

I am reminded of a Buddhist meal prayer that begins "This food is the gift of the whole universe—the earth, the sky, and much hard work." Those new to writing and art, like me with calligraphy, tend to want to forego the "hard work" part and skip to the meal. But there is no nourishment in that food.

A book, a vase, a painting—each has its own cycle. Sometimes no matter the quality of the seed or the care of the field, the hail comes and destroys the crop and we go hungry. But the season turns and we harness the horse again and hook up the plow. What we thought might take one season to come to fruition may take three or four or ten. Others might label our labor useless, or say we should give up and move to a different climate, but this is part of hard work and of life on the edge.

The hard work of writing entails showing up, practicing, and learning and applying the elements of craft. The work proceeds to revision, letting the writing rest, and exposing it to criticism. We repeat this sequence over and over again.

If we are writers, we keep writing and keep learning. We do not ever give up.

iii. Crafting the Writer

Early in our writing life, we tend to give our power away by accepting every critical comment as truth. We can learn to strain criticism from outside sources like a whale does plankton. Like this giant creature sieving the whole sea for nourishment, we strain the criticism for the gem that will make our writing better. When we perceive an attack, it is natural to want to defend ourselves and our work. The desire to defend, however, often comes from resistance to some truth we already know and do not want to accept. The more a comment annoys us, the more likely we need to listen for the grain of truth within it. The more we practice straining criticism through our own awareness, the more refined our discernment becomes.

Greater enemies to our confidence than the criticism of others, however, exist within our own minds—voices of comparison and judgment as well as those distracting us from the paper and pen. To craft ourselves as writers requires noticing and countering the inner voices that positively or negatively influence our beliefs and actions in relation to our work.

Listening to the Voices

One day, I typed WRITE! on my computer calendar. Every morning after that a little box popped up and reminded me to write. The box offered me three options: Open Item, Snooze, or Dismiss. Every morning, pushed to take care of business, I chose "Dismiss." Several weeks went by before the importance of what I was doing hit me. Dismiss? I was dismissing my writing, one of my greatest loves, with a tap of my finger, not thinking twice about what I was doing.

I sublimated my will and desire to write by placing priority on e-mail, banking, and Internet research. These tasks, while necessary, were not urgent. To reclaim my intention to write, I could have called on the attributes of the positive masculine to identify essentials and prioritize tasks. Using these attributes would have allowed me to focus on the work at hand and permit events to unfold in a natural sequence. If I had listened to direction from the positive masculine, I would have viewed my writing *as* my work instead of something in addition to my work.

I had succumbed to the voice of the negative masculine, the part of myself that defines success as productivity and uses linear tasks and technology as lures to distract me from the risky work of fulfilling my dreams. This voice convinces us to remain unconscious, to skim the surface of our lives so we can avoid the inner searching needed to thrive.

The negative masculine makes false claims that something "out there" that is fast and easy to obtain will not only make us happy but rich—the two supreme values of American culture. He argues that because the goal of writing is publication, we should simply follow the ten steps to a blockbuster novel, or adopt whatever method the newest how-to-publish handbook offers. "Why bother to write deeply, scouring your shadow side and raising your consciousness in the process, when the result of such effort will be hard to sell?" his voice admonishes.

Information technology is one of his favorite lures. Once, writers wrote in the nude or had servants chain them to their desks so they could not avoid writing. Now no escape from the world exists, even in our homes, unless we apply discipline and erect artificial barriers such as writing by hand, turning off the telephone, and disconnecting the Internet.

On another day, I might have been seduced by the voice of the negative feminine reminding me of my need to put others before myself. Her lists of *shoulds* can rule our social interactions. We say yes when we need to say no to sustaining relationships that do not nurture us. She suggests that our time would be better spent shopping, cooking, cleaning, or attending to the dramas of family, friends, or the pretend lives on television or in *People* magazine. The line between her *shoulds* and our own needs and obligations is not so easily drawn. When do we need to pay attention to the realities of sustaining relationships with friends and family and when is our inability to say no a drain on our writing?

The positive feminine answers the question simply: only a well-fed soul can offer sustenance to others. Through affirming rather than denying the self, we give conscious recognition to the legitimacy and meaningfulness of the many ways we serve in the world. Identification of the negative voices of both masculine and feminine allows us to invite their positive counterparts to the fore. The negative voices may enter our awareness unbidden, but we can choose not to follow their lead. Unless we learn to recognize and shun the negative voices by relying on the positive ones, we will forever be chasing, rather than fulfilling, our creative dream. Silence and solitude will elude us and interfere with the care and keeping of body, soul, mind, and spirit.

Seeking Light

By participating in writing "workshopping," we develop discernment as well as craft. Such workshops, generally led by a published writer, have the purpose of critically analyzing the work of each member. These groups differ from writing practice circles because they focus on crafting the results of our practice into a product. Workshopping is usually a component of any creative writing class. Workshopping is a common part of summer writing programs like the Breadloaf Writers Conference in Vermont and the Iowa Writing Workshop and provide the core of MFA creative writing programs.

Workshopping is also the function of critique groups, which are usually smaller and may not have a credentialed writer as leader. They often meet in living rooms, book-

The true gift of the workshopping experience lies in the opportunity it provides to develop individual authorial sensibility—the inner authority to discern the quality and value of our own work.

stores, and libraries rather than under the auspices of educational institutions. Critique groups have the added value of being ongoing and thereby provide an external structure for creating products regularly.

The true gift of the workshopping experience lies in the opportunity to develop authorial sensibility—the inner authority to discern the quality and value of our own work. In workshops, we unconsciously assimilate craft while we read manuscripts, write, listen to feedback of each person's piece, and selectively read the notes others write on ours. This assimilation provides an understanding beyond that gleaned from lectures, assigned readings, or writing exercises.

Two years ago, my husband discovered a volunteer dogwood in the wooded area behind our house. In the shade of the surrounding oaks and hickories, it looked fragile and bent by its search for sun. He staked it to provide support. Last year he read an article advising against such staking. Apparently the tree requires the jostling of the wind to develop stronger roots and a sturdy trunk. The tree also needs the freedom to find its own way to the light. He removed the stake.

When we engage in workshopping, we leave behind whatever support has nurtured our writing into being and agree to be buffeted by the winds of criticism. How we give and receive criticism tests our strength and our belief in our writing and in ourselves. In our journey toward our own authority, this skill, more than any other, measures how far we have come.

Workshopping can foster ego growth as easily as a dank bathroom fosters mold. Given the power to criticize, some feel compelled to wield it ruthlessly. This kind of power demeans and belittles, often in subtle and insidious ways. Women who have felt voiceless and powerless can become scathing critics under the guise of helping through correction.

Such criticism can devastate, even kill, the creative spirit. Alternatively, women sometimes avoid giving criticism by lapsing into kind generalities, which, though less psychologically harmful, provide no useful feedback to the writer.

Writing is more than linear thought, more than beautiful words. Writing is a way to pass on a thread of meaning that we have teased out of the tapestry of life.

Men can monopolize a mixed-gender group, often competing with one another, demeaning the women, and using hubris as a weapon. Women tend to defend themselves by withdrawing or using coquettish humor. An all-woman group may resist giving or receiving criticism by collapsing into a social or support group. These behaviors underscore the need for a strong leader who is knowledgeable in writing, self-aware, and skillful in group process. Without such grounding, the leader may use position and status to impose his or her will on class members, or give up authority and allow the purpose and focus of the group to be lost. If a teacher has rigid views defining "good writing," members may find themselves writing to please him or her, changing their style for the reward of a positive comment. As women, we often give our power to outer authority and depend on that authority for the measure of the worth of our work in this and many other instances.

By staying aware, we can discern where we stand in relationship to all these dynamics. An author has authority over her own work, and women especially must learn to claim it. We claim our authority by trusting our voice, our writing, and ourselves. Then we stand like a tree with our roots in solid ground, our arms open to the sky. From this position we are able to say no when an agent tells us to change our manuscript to meet current trends, and we are able to move on when the promised contract does not arrive and no one returns our calls. We can stand behind our work when it is criticized because we know it was as true and as good as we could make it when we wrote it. By the time we have completed a manuscript we are changed, just as the manuscript is changed from our original concept of it.

Writing is more than linear thought, more than beautiful words. Writing is a way to pass on a thread of meaning that we have teased out of the tapestry of life. We have no control over what others project onto our work. What carries us is like an undertow, invisible but strong and persistent, pulling us away from where we think safety lies. Our survival depends on submitting to the current, allowing it to carry us out to sea. There we find release and can make our way once again to shore.

Two Tibetan Buddhist teachers went out on a hillside and sat together in silence. After a long period, one turned to the other and said, pointing, "And they call that a tree!" Both men burst out laughing until their students saw them, like two orange balls, rolling in the grass with hilarity.

I heard this story several times without comprehension. Then one early spring day at a silent retreat I waited in line for dinner. I looked out the window and focused on a small plum tree showing the first signs of buds. The line was slow, the wait long. I inched forward, eyes on the tree until I no longer saw the tree but the universe. All of life was present in this tree. Me, the earth, all the constellations tied inexplicably to this young fragile tree. Then, no separation. I was the tree, the constellations. There were no boundaries, only emptiness.

And they call this a tree?

I did not understand the meaning so much as my body filled with it. Then the moment was gone.

EIGHT

Standing Out in My Field

The essential ingredient of the soul's journey through
affliction is the experience of social rejection.

— Helen Luke

One in twenty thousand Americans has six toes on one foot, doesn't wear underwear, makes a six-figure income, remembers life on a farm, commits suicide, or tries to, is a transvestite or transsexual, attends church regularly, reads pornography, owns a Mercedes.

I often feel like one in forty thousand Americans, like the burl knot on the walnut tree, the two-headed frog. An anomaly, a statistical variation too far out to even be computed. Like Pluto maybe, which astronomers have determined is not a real planet but a piece of debris from some exploding star, its orbit not a smooth ellipsis, but a weaving meander among the true planets.

Nineteen in twenty Americans do not know what I am talking about, would not stop to see the stars, and only one in a hundred thousand has slept on the desert floor trying to see the space where stars are not. Nineteen in twenty Americans eat at McDonald's; one in twenty is a vegetarian.

Why are we compelled by numbers? Nineteen in twenty Americans vainly seek reassurance of what normal is so they can fit into that particular piece of the pie-shaped graph. Are they missing the beauty of the large mole or the crooked tooth or the eye that wanders off to the left seeing everything perfectly?

i. Seeking Pasture

Surveying the Territory

To be a creative, we must be willing to stand out in our field and graze on our own grass. At what point we arrive at our willingness to do this depends on when the aridity of our lives drives us inward. Caitlin, a young woman in her early twenties, delves into her life mindful of the search and wary of the cultural enticements of money, fame, and possessions. She is an artist and writer; she has chosen to stay single for now.

Caitlin lives a *lento tempo* life. She seeks the company of older women perhaps because they support her choice to treat this time of her life as her "retirement." They speak of things that matter to her—self-fulfillment and creativity and inner searching. She says she has little in common with most women her own age. Even though she sometimes lives on the edge financially, she feels secure, sensing that if she follows her intuition, she will be taken care of and supported. It works, mainly because Caitlin is true to herself. Though she has occasional self-doubt, she does not doubt the path she has chosen—her version of the hero's journey.

In myth, the hero's journey is one of individuation. The hero, a male, hears a call, leaves home (separation), meets and overcomes obstacles in the external world (initiation), and arrives back home (return) transformed. Attempts have been made to adapt the hero's journey to women. Jungian Maureen Murdock suggests, however, that the story of a woman's heroic journey is only now being written—written by women like Caitlin.

Pulling Weeds

The Observer is the inner witness that observes while we write, listens as we chat with friends, and accompanies us wherever we go—whether or not we notice. Unlike the conscience of our childhoods, the Observer never judges, compares, or analyzes. The Observer only witnesses. It allows us to see what we are doing at the same time we are doing it. No shame, embarrassment, guilt, or judgment. The first time it made itself known to me, I was arguing with my husband when an almost audible line went through my head: "Look at how you do this." I stopped mid-tirade. Again: "It is a choice." To my husband I said, "Let's talk later," and left the room.

To be a writer, I had to become self-full. This is where the struggle lies, not in taking another class, earning an MFA, getting published, being a household name, or earning a huge advance for a book. The struggle is in being ourselves.

One of many things the Observer can do for us as writers is enhance our awareness of the voices that stop us from writing: voices of comparison (I can never be as good as she is) and of defense (I'm sure they turned it down because they don't want stories set in Poland). It points out how we deflect praise by belittling ourselves and how we apologize for our art. It shows us that our limitations are self-imposed.

The Observer begs us to stand beside it to look at what we are doing so we can see where it will lead us. "It is a choice," it says. With my husband, the choice was between peace and conflict, two paths that lead to different ends. What did I really want?

To know what we want, we have only to watch what we do. This relates to wanting to write. Usually phrased as "I want to write, *but…*"

My personal story goes like this. I wrote on the job, in a notebook and in a journal, and did not consider myself a writer. I published and did not consider myself a writer. I could say, "I write," but could not say, "I am a writer." When I finally wrote "writer" on a tax form in the space beside "occupation," I expected to be arrested by the IRS or the FBI. Seriously.

The Observer watched all this while nodding its cloud-like head. "Very interesting," it noted. "Look at how you do *that*!" It also began to show me that writing was not separate from my life, that the walls I had erected to give myself the illusion of safety not only kept me from fulfilling my desire to write, they kept me *from* life. The Observer helped me see how I had seen writing as a goal that only the "special" could reach. I knew I was not special, having integrated the messages of childhood about taking up too much space, blowing my own horn, being conceited, and showing off. How could I be a writer with these voices in my head? How could I be selfish enough, conceited enough, self-absorbed enough to remain still and receptive, open to what writing asked of me?

Yet, how could I not, when I felt a voice within surging up, wanting expression? My frustration at what seemed an impasse was huge, causing me to lash out angrily at those I loved and to take bizarre risks out of some deep adolescent naiveté. I did not know what I wanted to say, but I perceived the world "out there" as stopping me. I looked for validation, but negated any praise with self-judgment.

To be a writer, I had to become self-full. This is where the struggle lies, not in taking another class, earning an MFA, getting published, being a household name, or earning a huge advance for a book.

The struggle is in being ourselves.

Praying for Rain

"Want" is both an expression of desire and of lack—the desire to fill some kind of emptiness. In order to fulfill the desire, we have to objectify it. To fill the desire for love, we envision our perfect lover; to fill the desire to write, we imagine what that looks like—usually in the form of fame and fortune. The Observer says, "Look at how you do *that*—how you make publication and recognition into goals to prove what is already true. Do you write? Well then, you are a writer."

Our wanting arises from self-doubt. We think publishing, acclaim, and fame will give us the self-assurance we lack. Instead, they give us more distraction and more to fear losing. For our writing to be truly ours, a pure expression of who we are in that moment, we must let go of the expectation of what writing might do for us in the future. Self-doubt rides with us in the passenger seat no matter where we go or who we are. We never banish self-doubt, we merely learn not to listen to it for direction. If we do, we will shift into reverse. What is important is to steer straight ahead and stay on the road. That is it. Stay on the road and see where we go. Then back on the road to the next stop, and the next, and the next. No destination, only an adventurous journey without a map.

We must play the edge, that place where all artists live. The seeming reality of the world pressures us about relationships, earning a living, being successful. But another reality whispers about being true to oneself, about inner being, about the power of art to change the world. Every human being lives on this edge, but very possibly, only artists and spiritual practitioners acknowledge where they stand. Most people have at least one foot solidly in the "real" world. Mystics and some people labeled as "crazy" live immersed in an other-worldly reality. The creative plays the edge between.

Playing the edge requires us to follow our own road and to give up worrying about the opinions and advice of others even when they are respected writers, agents, or friends. Following our own rhythm requires listening to the body's wisdom by accessing the unconscious and following intuition. Standing out in our field is isolating and unconventional. It is also freeing. When Kris Kristofferson defined freedom as "nothing left to lose" in the song *Me and Bobby McGee*, he defined a necessity of

We are not writing a good story or intriguing ideas, we are manifesting a part of ourselves in three-dimensional reality as surely as if we were birthing a child. This is not a metaphor; it is what creatives do.

creative process—to move ahead unfettered by fear of loss.

In Western society in the twenty-first century, so much emphasis is placed on commercial success that the essence of art and literature could be lost. Faced with a book of literary quality, an agent might request steamier sex or recommend a new plot line for the author to follow. Commercial writers can write to such specifications and have no qualms about doing so. For others of us, however, our *wanting* is to write first from ourselves and then consider the market, rather than the other way around. *Never allow money or notoriety to drive your writing* advises author Ray Bradbury. He goes on to suggest that writing for love is a better solution—for love and the joy of work.

ii. Storm Warnings

"To control your cow, give it a wide pasture." Shunryu Suzuki's words, like many Zen masters' sayings, tell us a great deal about the paradox of being a writer or other creative. Like a cow, our writing needs to be held in a wide space, the size and shape of which only we can determine from our intimate knowledge of its needs. We glean this knowledge by observing ourselves.

I am always learning more about my creative process. In writing this book, I have discovered that my most fruitful writing time is from ten to twelve in the morning. I can write for about two hours and produce fresh, meaningful prose. Before I begin writing, I meditate, exercise, and structure business or personal items I need to address later in the day. After morning writing, if I go for a walk or read or rest, I can come back to writing for another two hours in the afternoon. In the past, I attempted to keep a strict first-thing-in-the-morning regimen—mainly because I had read this is how famous—mostly male—writers worked. Although a rigid structure works for me when applied to edits and revisions, I understand now that for my writing to flow, allowing is more important than scheduling.

We are responsible for the care and keeping of our writing. Perhaps one of the hardest things to learn is when the pull away from the process means a need for gestation as opposed to being a distraction from something we want to avoid. The only way to learn this, however, is to write, observe what we do, and listen to our bodies tell us why. As women, especially, we need space for the discovery of our own process. Only we can give ourselves that space.

We are not writing a good story or intriguing ideas, we are manifesting a part of ourselves in three-dimensional reality as surely as if we were birthing a child. This is not a metaphor; it is what creatives do.

Sensitive to relationship, we sense the energetic and physical sameness between creating a child and creating a book. Our inner knowing understands, as does the body. But there is no cultural context for this birthing, no recognition other than dollar signs for this bond. Once the book is born, what happens can be wrenching. The publication/marketing system prizes the book while giving little attention to the author. The system may propose that the book be rewritten to attract buyers. Do we agree to the changes to ensure publication, or do we hold out to preserve the book's message?

If we put our writing first, we will not be so easily lured away from what really matters to us. This is why we need to write for the love of writing, not for fame, fortune, admiration, or other external gratification. The gratification must be inner, derived from the simple act of putting pen to paper, one word after the other. Writing is an art many people can engage in successfully as long as "successful" is self-defined. Write for the pure joy of telling the story. Time enough to ask what next.

iii. Four Paradoxes

Reading the Signs

When does some become too much, or when is some too little? Which drop of rain causes the flood, which hour of sunshine a drought? When I suggested an antidote to a friend's unhappiness, she replied, "I wouldn't know who I was if I weren't unhappy." At what moment had she chosen that identity?

Writers commonly focus on the suffering endured for the sake of art. The struggle to find time, the inane questions of non-writers who do not understand, the rejection from agents and publishers—we speak of all of this and more in tones of despair. Under the despair, however, can run a kind of pride in our specialness. Who would we be without our angst as artists? Are we clinging to suffering while striving to avoid it?

Four paradoxes comprise our ceaseless striving to avoid suffering: pleasure and pain, praise and criticism, fame and disgrace, and gain and loss. In Buddhism, these pairs are called the Eight Worldly Dharmas or teachings. I find it useful to think about these teachings in relation to the writing life. Note that there is no crayon-thick black line between each pair, or between one pair and the next. As a result, each pair presents a paradox, one that cannot be resolved outside the moment.

Paradox One: Pleasure and Pain

Pleasure and pain can be seen as getting what we want and avoiding getting what we do not want. We derive pleasure from writing or we would not write. At some point, we have been rewarded, perhaps by the simple joy of self-expression in a journal or diary, or the magic of discovering what we think by putting pen to paper. Others may also have rewarded us—teachers, parents, friends. But as women, especially when young, with our innate desire for and dependence on support through relationship, we are particularly vulnerable to the withdrawal of support. If we are dependent on the good opinion of others, then our fragile dreams can come crashing down. Many women in my classes had quit writing or quit sharing their writing early in life because of a negative opinion expressed by someone important to them.

Each time we set words on paper, we can feel the pain of our inadequate words, knowing the meaning lies in the white space around the black lines.

To experience the pleasure of writing, we must explore the pain in our own psyches. We may think we can avoid psychic pain by focusing on nonfiction, such as journalism or research, something concrete and rational. But whatever our fears in relation to our work, they are sure to materialize somewhere in our lives. As the adage goes: what we resist, persists. The more we avoid evoking our fear, the more insidious it becomes, even inserting itself into our dreams.

Beneath the fear of reopening wounds of the past lies further paradox. Pleasure and joy abound when the words flow. We sense a rhythm as palpable as it is elusive. We cannot force this flow. It appears or does not. When it does not, we can feel as dead as the prose sounds. We are at the mercy of the Muse who seems particularly fickle, disappearing when we need her most. The fear of losing her entirely pierces our hearts.

Each time we set words on paper, we can feel the pain of our inadequate words, knowing the meaning lies in the white space around the black lines. We must trust readers to understand, although we know the words fall short. Other writers, those judged successful and famous, say the same—the book as written never quite measures up to the book intended. Still we return to the page again and again, not because we believe this time will be different, but because we are writers and can do nothing else.

When the book or story is finished, the pleasure of creation diminishes and we may lapse into depression or despair or grief. A great emptiness descends like that when a loved one dies. Fear arises that we will never again be able to write, that no one will read our work even if we have both agent and publisher, and that we will wallow in the pain of self-doubt and self-pity forever. When we read the lives of revered and famous writers, we discover we are not alone in this experience.

Paradox Two: Praise and Criticism

Praise and criticism refer to wanting praise for our abilities and not wanting attention placed on our shortcomings. Like children, we want dessert with no responsibility for the nutritional needs of our bodies. Like children, we carry extraordinary sensitivity to humiliation and ridicule.

The paradox is that we ask for and need feedback while fearing it. When praise is given, we often question its sincerity or fear its withdrawal. When suggestions for improvement are offered, we may want to defend ourselves and discount the offer of help. Unless we come to

The more difficult we find the experience of separating from our creations—whether our children, our homes, or our art—the more likely we are to take praise and criticism personally.

terms with how we deal with praise and criticism, we can learn nothing. We cannot improve or grow; we cannot learn the discernment and discrimination we need to assess what feedback to accept and what to reject.

The more difficult we find the experience of separating from our creations—whether our children, our homes, or our art—the more likely we are to take praise and criticism personally. If we were subjected to blame in childhood, we are susceptible to integrating criticism of our work as criticism of our very being. A writer of memoir may feel particularly threatened, as if her life rather than her writing is on the line. We women can easily give our power to those we deem more informed, talented, or trained. This is why, in a writing practice circle, the leader writes and reads with the group. She has two roles: to create a safe, supportive circle for writing and to model risk-taking and fearlessness.

A writing circle consists of peers. Each woman, including the leader, brings contributions of equal value even while each has different experience and expertise. The leader demonstrates how to ride the waves of "good" and "poor" writing. In addition, by emphasizing "what works" in each person's writing, the leader gently nudges each writer toward her own voice. Criticism tempts us to conform to the opinion and values of the critic. To create, we must depend on our own values. A good leader shows us the way to clarify those values for ourselves.

Neither praise nor criticism should be accepted without scrutiny. Praise is sometimes flattery in disguise, or is given by someone reluc-

179

tant to provide honest, though critical, feedback. Usually, however, error is made on the side of the negative. Humans have a tendency, when given permission to critique, to apply a ruthless pencil, as if by making someone else look small we will look bigger.

Paradox Three: Fame and Disgrace

Fame and disgrace refer to the desire for public acclaim and avoidance of anonymity. In a very real sense, the cultural emphasis on fame and money as symbols of literary success threatens the art of writing itself, especially the writing of women. I agree with Helen Luke, who said that a woman in touch with her soul cannot write for money alone, and that the need to abandon her inner process to seek public notice for her book can be a kind of suicide.

On the simplest level, we want our writing read and appreciated. Many of us first come to writing circles expressing satisfaction with writing for ourselves or our families. As we gain confidence and skill, however, we often turn to fiction or creative nonfiction and aim for publication. I have never met anyone who does not point to publication with pride, even if her work is a single-paragraph letter to the editor.

Most of us joke about hitting the bestseller list, being interviewed on *Good Morning America,* and winning the Pulitzer or Newbery or Edgar, but our humor is only a thin veil over a real desire. We would love to prove wrong the people who told us we could not make a living writing. We want to find our name used as answers to crossword clues and in literary columns in the *New York Times.* We build an imaginary world of important people, exotic places, and money to support us as we write further great works.

The truth is that success and acclaim bring their own terrors. The spotlight offers to blind us, to provide us with a persona we have never donned before. Will we accept the cape of specialness and forget who we really are? The curtains of fame can part easily to expose our deepest vulnerabilities.

In January 2005 on PBS's *The McLaughlin Group*, host Jim McLaughlin asked panel members how each thought history would view George W. Bush. Conservative columnist Pat Buchanan said, "As a tragic figure." My political views fell away for the moment and revealed to me a human being who, having risen or been pushed to the height of fame and power, would later shrivel into an object of pity, whether brought on by himself or others or both.

The possibility of a fall from grace highlights the paradox of fame and disgrace: if our egos are dependent on believing we *are* what we have become acclaimed for, then we live in terror of discovery as the imposters we fear we are.

On a small scale, even the two-book contract can contain a trap. Elated to have sold a manuscript, an author grasps the opportunity of an advance on a second book. Such contracts usually require delivering the manuscript within one year. While some writers thrive on deadlines, others find their creative juices drying up. In addition, most writers spend years on the first book. The quality of a book produced in a single year rarely lives up to the first effort that may have taken ten. Therein lie disappointment and the possibility of ignominy or oblivion.

The writing life seems rife with opportunities for humiliation, public and private. No one comes to the book signing, few show up for a lecture. Rejection slips pile up like snow before a plow. Fame can have equally devastating effects, especially on relationships. Not only do we not know what we will find, we are unsure who will stay with us and whom we will leave behind. Family members, thinking they see themselves in our writing, quit speaking to us. Acquaintances ask for sales figures or how the book is coming, and we have to mumble something in return. Some people put us on a pedestal so that authentic friends become hard to find. Those we relied on when we struggled may turn their backs or actively betray us.

The answer to the paradox of fame and disgrace lies in learning to stand alone with who we are at our innermost core. In that stance, we stand steady in the waves of either fame or disgrace. We focus on our own integrity and the integrity of our work, and let the rest wash over us. Not that this is easy or simple or without pain; but to be an artist, it is what we must do.

Paradox Four: Gain and Loss

Gain and loss, the desire for comfort and happiness and avoidance of discomfort and unhappiness, provide the final paradox. We equate change with discomfort while at the same time desiring things to be different than they are.

On many levels, the creative's journey is a slow stripping away of all that is unessential. First, the stripping of externals—those relationships, jobs, social obligations, and hobbies that distract us from our work in the moment and hinder us from attending to the ongoing hum of our creative process. Second, the stripping of internals—the entrenched attitudes and judgments that penetrate our words, while arousing our resistance to self-exposure. A refusal to engage in internal examination hinders our creative progress.

While we find ourselves afraid of spelunking into unknown depths, growing to maturity and coming of age to our creative selves require leaving the old self behind. We write to discover what we think and who we are, and as a result, our writing changes us.

Through writing, we gain a perspective of ourselves as explorers of what is, as prospectors searching for who we can be, and as pilgrims seeking the ineffable. No way exists to make this gain other than to accept that discomfort, anxiety, and insecurity are necessary. We consent to uneasiness as motivation for the creative journey—which is no less than our spiritual journey toward self-realization. Although ever aware of the hundreds of roads not taken, at our deepest core we know that this road is truly the only one we could have trod.

I am a child of the Colorado Desert, a vast expanse of flat barren land in southeastern California. Occasionally my parents would take my older sister and me to a friend's fish camp on Lake Havasu, the reservoir for Parker Dam. The cabin there consisted of a plywood platform with four hardboard walls nailed to upright posts. Overhead beams held up a plywood roof. After my father checked for rattlesnakes, he allowed us to follow him up the wooden ladder. We would clamber over the low parapet and roll out our sleeping bags on iron cots fitted with stained, blue-ticked mattresses. Beneath a sky more stars than night, we listened to coyotes sing, kangaroo rats scurry across the sand, and the occasional bray of wild burros. In the morning before rising, we'd shake our shoes for scorpions and look under our beds for snakes. These were some of the daily perils of desert living.

My desert provides the ground of my writing, not because I write about it, but because the desert infiltrated my being, becoming the internal landscape where I stand alone. Spaciousness. A place where beauty must be sought in the shifting shadows of sand and nothing can be taken for granted.

Not another soul saw that carpet of stars from the roof of the fish camp like I did. Not even my sister lying beside me. While I stand out in my field alone, I alone have the story of that field to tell, and I am changed in the telling of it. To write, I am forced to leave my tribe and become the prospector, the pilgrim, the explorer. By accepting these appellations and their roles, I submit to the ultimate solitude and discomfort, discovery and joy, of my creative journey.

NINE

Sliding Down the Great Mother's Breast

I am slowly, painfully discovering that my refuge is not found in my mother, my grandmother, or even the birds of Bear River. My refuge exists in my capacity to love. If I can learn to love death then I can begin to find refuge in change.

— *Terry Tempest Williams*

We birthed her. Like a team of midwives, we guided her through the maze of her becoming. We wiped her forehead, smoothed her hair, and held a damp rag to her parched lips. We lifted her to her feet when she said, "Up! Up!" until her son held her in his arms, swaying to music only the two of them could hear. We sat, sang, massaged, chanted, and prayed.

In turn, we'd say, "Go to the Mother."

"Push out through your crown."

"Let go. Let go."

I reminded her of a dream she'd had in which she was told she knew how to die, that it is as easy as sliding down the Great Mother's breast.

At last the moment came. A quiet breath, a long silence, a deep sigh. She was gone.

The six of us women left the room so her son and partner could be alone with her.

"What do we do now?" one asked.

"We could wash her body," I said.

The others didn't respond to my suggestion until I repeated it.

"I don't know how to do this. I've never done it before," one woman said.

"I haven't either," I said, "but our bodies must remember—women have done this for thousands of years."

I ran water in a basin. Someone added an essential oil and another found washcloths. We washed her body and anointed it with lotion while we sang and chanted. I selected a green dress patterned with roses, perfect for burial in the arms of Mother Earth. I combed her hair. Another placed flowers in her hands.

Later, as I left the hospice, I saw movement beneath a small dogwood tree, its boughs heavy with red-tipped flowers. A newly emerged moth, large and velvety brown with circles like eyes on its moist wings, fluttered on the pine mulch readying itself for flight. I watched for a long time, hoping to ensure its safety.

Knowing I couldn't, I left before it flew away.

i. The Leap into Emptiness

Death of an Artist

My friend Temple was an artist of intuitive paintings of the goddess in all of her myriad forms. Environmental illness drove her to use this mode of painting as a path to physical healing. She struggled with her art. She feared the reaction people would have to her paintings, which she roughly classified as "naked women with bloody vaginas." Her paintings were much more than that, but she resisted showing or selling. She blamed lack of money—to have time to paint, she worked part-time and lived on the edge financially. I noted, however, that each time she decided to have a show, torpor would overtake her, and she would jettison her plans.

When she was diagnosed with lymphoma in December 2003, Temple went on disability and depended on Medicaid to pay for healthcare. She rejected allopathic medicine and decided against chemotherapy. She wanted alternative treatment, but had no means to pay for it. With this impetus, she decided to sell her paintings. From her bed at the hospice and with the help of friends, she orchestrated an art show, a focused activity that energized her and, those of us around her felt, kept her alive.

The more difficult we find the experience of separating from our creations—whether our children, our homes, or our art—the more likely we are to take praise and criticism personally.

The show was both a glorious and tragic event. She came in her wheelchair with her oxygen tank. She saw her paintings hung on the creamy walls of a nineteenth-century mansion and received the accolades her work richly deserved from the many friends and strangers gathered. The show was a financial success. All the originals and many prints were sold. She was ready to ride peacefully out in a blaze of glory as the artist she had never quite had the courage or strength to be while healthy.

Coincidentally, each of the three of us who formed her primary care team had plans to leave town shortly after the show. This news gave Temple the courage to face what she had been denying: she was dying. This admitted, she wanted our threesome with her. She orchestrated her death much as she had the art show, even calling a circle of witnesses to her bedside in the middle of the night for a kind of dress rehearsal two days later before the final event.

She died four months after her initial diagnosis, the time period predicted by one of her dreams. The money from the art sales paid for her funeral and her burial in Asheville's historic Riverside Cemetery. She lies close to the grave of Thomas Wolfe and not far from William Sydney Porter (O. Henry), who both shared with her the struggles innate to creative minds and lives.

I saw myself in Temple's fear of having her art rejected. I saw how I held back, sat on the fence, turned off the encouragement of others, and clung to self-disparagement as an excuse not to create. I also had let torpor overtake me and blamed lack of finances and my need to earn a living. I knew, as I believe Temple did, that these external reasons were subterfuge. The true fear lies in the awareness that beyond the door we must pass through to claim our art is empty space.

Years ago I had a dream in which my friend Sylvia was writing a newsletter on my computer. She called Teijo Munnich, a Soto Zen teacher, and me to help her because each time she finished typing a page, the words disappeared. Perplexed, we watched this happen again and again until Teijo said, "I know why it's doing that—the truth cannot be revealed in words. The truth is revealed in emptiness."

If we love the truth enough to seek it out, we must agree to live with uncertainty and discomfort and quit pretending that safety and security are possible in this world.

I do not know what will happen when I sit down to write or when I arise from writing, when I send off the manuscript or when I get the response in the mail, when the book is published or remaindered or made into a movie. I also do not know if I will live to eat my next meal.

The same urge that pulls me into creative process repels me. Speaking on the subject of meditation, Buddhist teacher Pema Chodron said, "We don't meditate to become better meditators. We meditate to become more aware of our lives." Similarly, when we write, we become more aware of our lives. In the process, we become better writers. When I write, I understand it is myself that will be revealed—not the self I have constructed to feel safe in my world, but a self I do not fully know. The promise of adventurous discovery provides both the impetus to move forward and the urge to run away. The truth is that whichever way I run, I will meet myself and the unknown.

To live the life of a creative, we, like the antelope in the African story, must seek safety by running straight toward the lion's roar with no certainty of the outcome. Still we take the risk. We face our weaknesses, the possibility of our death, over and over again. Vulnerability to danger—most probably in the forms of distraction, comparison, fear, and self-doubt—is an occupational hazard. Coexistence with our predators is the price we pay to graze among the tall grasses and drink at the waterhole. The nature of that coexistence, however, is up to us.

Although women have an innate capacity to tolerate not knowing, we do not embrace it willingly. We want to write because we have written and touched the spaciousness. While the promise of this experience lures us on, we understand that to create we must destroy. If we are to be writers, then we must submit to our annihilation. If we love the truth enough to seek it out, we must agree to live with uncertainty and discomfort and quit pretending that safety and security are possible in this world.

ii. Befriending Ourselves

Fear is an inevitable fellow traveler on the creative journey. When fear settles next to us, it alerts us to possibility and to growth. To be writers, we must understand that we cannot write on the surface of things, but must dive deep into unknown waters in search of our own truth. If we deny fear or try to circumvent it, our writing will lack feeling and imagination, and we will fail to touch the universality of experience to reach our readers.

Once I had a dream in which I kept my baby upstairs in my home. I knew it needed food and attention, but I was too occupied on the main level of the house with my husband and business. The baby died. I was guilty and grief-stricken. The dream was a warning that I was in danger of killing my creative life and my higher consciousness for the sake of my business and a place in the outer world. My feminine self— the nurturer, soul searcher, and creator—had abandoned its meaning and purpose and was no longer supporting life.

In another dream, I met a man and his five-year-old granddaughter in an airport. I bonded deeply with this beautiful child and told the man I would not know what to do if she were mine because my love for her was so deep and boundless, so unconditional and encompassing, my heart did not feel big enough to hold it. The child represented my innermost self whom I have not always honored or acknowledged. Our relationship with our writing needs the same nurturance as that with our children and lovers. If we value our writing, we spend time with it: we make it a priority in our lives. When we lose contact with our creative selves, our bodies remind us—through dreams, illness, or injury that force us to be still and solitary.

iii. Tree, Tree, Tree

Temple loved the old-growth trees. Several times during her illness she asked to be taken where she could sit propped against a tree's trunk. She was pleased that from her bed at the hospice, she could see a large hemlock.

Fred Rogers, the award-winning educator, minister, and television host of *Mr. Rogers' Neighborhood*, died during Temple's hospice stay. A local man who had attended seminary with Rogers wrote to the newspaper telling the story of a discussion the two had as students. Rogers said that it did not matter what words we used, if we said them with love, then that was enough. He insisted that you could say "tree, tree, tree" with love and affect people's lives. The man had shared Rogers' idea with his wife, and "tree, tree, tree" became their family's password for "I love you." They wrote it on notes to tuck into family lunch pails and suitcases, or under pillows. They and their children felt free to say the words wherever they happened to be, even to shout them across parking lots and airport terminals.

I took the story to Temple. Soon "tree, tree, tree" was heard along the hospice corridor as friends and nurses came and went. Inside Temple's room the words were spoken often, including as a blessing over a friend's pregnant belly.

Surrender to the creative process, like dying, is a solitary leap into emptiness. We practice taking this leap over and over again, reshaping ourselves and refining our souls.

One day, I sat with Temple, the two of us looking out at the hemlock. I was there and we were alone so that I could encourage her to tell me her wishes for her body, her commemoration, and other details concerning her impending death. Periodically she would laugh and shake her head. "It's really weird having this conversation with you."

I agreed. It certainly was not a conversation I wanted to be having, but I was the only one she would allow past her resistance and denial. She wanted to be interred, but not embalmed. She suggested a plain pine casket and grew animated when I suggested that her friends paint the casket using her technique of intuitive painting.

"Is there anything you want on the headstone besides your name and dates?"

With a mischievous glint in her eyes, she flashed her broad smile and told me her wish. So it is that visitors to Asheville's Riverside Cemetery who wander past the mausoleums on the hill behind Thomas Wolfe's grave will find, to their great puzzlement, a tombstone engraved: TREE TREE TREE. Perhaps they think it refers to the sugar maples at the foot of her plot.

"It's a great honor to be asked to witness someone's dying," my friend Susan Trout once told me. I know this is true. I also know that with honor comes responsibility. We are responsible to be present and openhearted, to be honest with ourselves and with those we serve. To tend the dying well requires surrender to the process and a willingness to be led both by the dying person and by our hearts. These same qualities are required of us as writers. That's what writing takes—everything we have.

iv. Practice Makes Possible

The Tibetan Buddhists use meditation and other spiritual tools to practice dying so that they might die consciously and well. Practitioners learn to face their fear of death, walking through it to liberation and higher states of consciousness.

Surrender to the creative process, like dying, is a solitary leap into emptiness. We practice taking this leap over and over again, reshaping ourselves and refining our souls. Each time we pick up the pen is an opportunity to shed another layer of the self that believes it knows how things are. We see through new eyes and with a new freedom of being. This process continues as long as we show up to write.

Here are some things for us to remember:

- ◎ Practice. Practice. Practice.
- ◎ Process before product.
- ◎ Writing requires silence, solitude, space, and the courage and awareness to search our shadow side.
- ◎ Write from the belly, not the brain; write from the heart, not the head.
- ◎ The body with its intuition and our willingness to listen to what the body says are our greatest assets as writers.
- ◎ Writing and publishing are not the same thing. If we write, we are writers. If we publish what we write, we are published writers. A published writer is not a better writer. A published writer is simply a writer who is published.
- ◎ We write for ourselves and to experience the transcendence of craft. When we are finished, we might send our work off to agents and publishers; then we go back to writing.
- ◎ We each receive our own answer, recognized intuitively, to the question of how to fit writing into our lives. We must listen to hear that answer.
- ◎ Following our intuition and being on our path does not mean the way will be easy, without obstacles, or comfortable.
- ◎ The company of other women makes the journey meaningful, instructive, and a lot more fun.
- ◎ No matter what we write, we cannot hide behind our words.
- ◎ One step at a time. That is the way of the feminine.
- ◎ Live lightly—laugh, rest, and love.
- ◎ Embrace silence and solitude.
- ◎ Befriend the shadow side.
- ◎ Process before product.
- ◎ Practice. Practice. Practice.

Writing—all art—has the power to transmute our self-limitations and enable us to redefine ourselves and our lives. Women creatives lead the way because, as creatives, we are the most in touch with the struggle between the outer and inner worlds, and because, as women, it is our time.

Writing is not such a different process from dying. Both processes require us to leap alone into the void with only faith as a net. We cannot choose whether to live or die. The choice lies in whether we live or die consciously and creatively.

Journey Without End

*It is the task of the writer ... to become, in the words of
Henry James, a person on whom nothing is lost. What
is put into the care of such a person will be well tended.
Such a person can be trusted to tell the stories she is
given to tell, and to tell them with the compassion that
comes when the self's deepest interest is not in the
self, but in turning outward and into awareness.*

— Jane Hirschfield

Staring into space,
I imagine my destiny, the gift of my life:
A long line of women in bright striped shawls
wend their way up a mountain;
they laugh and cry,
they sing old songs, hold hands.
Each carries a basket of words
and approaches where I stand by the altar.
One by one, each sprinkles her words
like petals across the crystal table,
and says,
These are my words,
all of myself,
I give to Lord Mother
from whom they came.
The words turn into diamonds,
the diamonds into water, and
the water into rivers
rushing down mountains to nourish the earth.
The women turn into trees and flowers and plants
to hold the earth together with their roots.
They sing in the wind—of truth, peace,
and all things warm and growing.

You ou know what is necessary. You know what you need to do.

Write from the heart. Be unafraid of your own truth even if it burns you. Keep your heart open with fierce compassion. Write even when you think you are not—remembering that a writer is always writing, even while gazing out the window, crying over fallen soldiers, or taking a child to the park.

"Love is a deep and a dark and a lonely," Carl Sandburg wrote. Writing is also that deep, that dark, and, oh yes, that lonely. But what does that matter to you? You are fearless. You are a woman able to stride through life like your grandmothers who were immigrants, displaced, pioneers, or enslaved; who may have been wealthy, poor, or middle class and abused or silenced, or too sheltered to know they should be afraid of the box-walls around them.

Are you scared? So be it. Remember how it feels to let the pen go. To be fearless. To be free. To release the anger, the fear, the worry, and denial. Recall the joy, the looseness, the liberty that come with the words. Lord Mother is the very earth you walk on. Use the energy she so generously gives you.

Fearlessness applies courage to the task of exploring your inner self. When you are fearless you recognize your vulnerability and find your strength in it. To be fearless is not "blind courage." Fearlessness *sees* the danger, accepts it, and draws strength from walking toward it.

I encourage you to run. Now. Run toward the lion's roar. Leap into the void. Freedom to discover and speak your truth calls from the other side. You can only discover who you can be as an individual and what we women are capable of as a collective if you move out of your comfort zone and explore the divine dissatisfaction that continually feeds your soul and your creativity.

Stand up straight. Own yourself. Claim your soul and its destiny. You are a writer. Nothing takes that away. Joyful word-making—that is what writing is. Joyful word-making, artful soul-making. Your journey to? Wherever it takes you. That's a promise I can make, because I am on that journey too. I will be watching as you scurry past or beside you as you make your way or ahead reaching back my hand and saying, "You can do it. You can voice your truth and survive. You can grow and change and burst the seams of past limitations. You can be the woman you have dreamed of being. Oh, yes. You can."

A dream—
A woman tells me, "You can no longer remain silent.
You can no longer bow your head in silence.
You must hold your head high and speak from the
deepest part of yourself.
Even in front of the king."

— Anne Scott

Will you do it? Will you?

— Bishop Desmond Tutu

Bibliography

Books Contributing to *Women, Writing, and Soul-Making*

Andreasen, Nancy. *The Creating Brain: The Neuroscience of Genius.* New York: Dana Press. 2005.

Beasley, Deena. "Fight vs. Flight. Study: Women Socialize Away Stress." ABC News. May 19, 2000. http://www.rafcom.co.uk/medical_dental/stress_women.cfm. Accessed June 1, 2000.

Bolen, Jean Shinoda. *Crossing to Avalon: A Woman's Midlife Quest for the Sacred Feminine.* San Francisco: HarperSanFrancisco, 1994.

_____. *Goddesses in Older Women: Archetypes in Women over Fifty.* New York: HarperCollins, 2001.

_____. *The Millionth Circle: How to Change Ourselves and the World.* Berkeley: Conari Press, 1999.

Bradbury, Ray. *Zen in the Art of Writing.* New York: Bantam, 1992.

Brande, Dorothea. *Becoming a Writer.* New York: Tarcher/Putnam, 1934.

Brehony, Kathleen A. *Awakening at Midlife: A Guide to Reviving Your Spirit, Recreating Your Life, and Returning to Your Truest Self.* New York: Riverhead Books, 1996.

Campbell, Joseph. *The Hero with a Thousand Faces.* Princeton: Princeton University Press, 1973.

Childre, Doc and Deborah Rozman. *Overcoming Emotional Chaos.* San Diego: Jodere Group, Inc., 2002.

de Mille, Agnes. *The Life and Work of Martha Graham.* New York: Random House, 1956, 1991.

Dillard, Annie. *Pilgrim at Tinker Creek.* New York: HarperPerennial Modern Classics, 1998.

_____. *The Writing Life.* New York: Harper & Row, 1989.

Doyle, Brian. "Leap: Remembering the Unimaginable, One Year After." *Utne Reader*, Sept.-Oct. 2002. Reprinted from *The American Scholar*, Winter 2002.

Duricy, Michael P. "Black Madonnas." http://campus.udayton.edu/mary/meditations/blackmdn.html. Accessed March 15, 2009.

Ensler, Eve. *The Vagina Monologues.* New York: Villard Books, 1998.

Estes, Clarissa Pinkola. *Women Who Run with the Wolves: Myths and Stories of the Wild Woman Archetype.* New York: Ballatine Books, 1992.

Fox, Matthew. "The Return of the Black Madonna: A Sign of Our Times or How the Black Madonna Is Shaking Us Up for the Twenty-First Century." 2006. http//www.matthewfox.org/systmpl/theblackmadonna. Accessed January 15, 2007.

Galland, China. *The Bond between Women: A Journey to Fierce Compassion.* New York: Riverhead Books, 1998.

_____. "Chartres and the Great Mystery of the Black Madonna," Blog Post #3, September 19, 2007, on Penguin Blog (USA). http://us.penguingroup.com/static/html/blogs/guest-author/ longing-darkness-china-galland. Accessed March 17, 2009.

_____. *Longing for Darkness: Tara and the Black Madonna.* New York: Penguin, 1990.

Gendlin, Eugene. *Focusing.* New York: Bantam New Age Book, 1981.

Greenspan, Miriam. *Healing Through the Dark Emotions: The Wisdom of Grief, Fear, and Despair.* Boston: Shambhala, 2003.

_____. "Wisdom in the Dark Emotions." *Shambhala Sun.* January, 1993.

_____. "Through a Glass Darkly: On Moving from Grief to Gratitude." *The Sun.* January, 2008: 4-11. Issue 385.

Heilbrun, Carolyn G. *Writing a Woman's Life.* New York: Ballantine Books, 2002.

_____. *Toward a Recognition of Androgyny: The First—and Still the Richest—Discussion of Androgyny and Its Implications.* New York: W.W. Norton, 1973.

Hawkins, David R. *Power vs. Force: The Hidden Determinants of Human Behavior.* New York: Hay House, 2002.

Hirshfield, Jane. *Nine Gates: Entering the Mind of Poetry.* New York: HarperPerennial, 1997.

Keats, John. *The Letters of John Keats*. H. Buxton Forman, Ed. NP: Kessinger Publishing, 2004.

Lakshmanan, Indira A.R. "Secret Chinese Language for Women is Dying Off." *Santa Cruz Sentinel*, reprinted from *The Boston Globe*. Wednesday, December 8, 1999.

Lehrer, Jonah. *Proust Was a Neuroscientist*. Boston: Houghton Mifflin, 2007.

Lorde, Audre. *The Cancer Journals: The Original Edition*. San Francisco: aunt lute books, 2006.

Luke, Helen M. *Sense of the Sacred: A Portrait of Helen M. Luke*. Videocassette. New York: Parabola Books, Sept. 1, 1999.

_____. *The Way of Woman: Awakening the Perennial Feminine*. New York: Doubleday, 1995.

Millin, Peggy Tabor. *Mary's Way: A Universal Story of Spiritual Growth Inspired by the Message of Medjugorje*. Berkeley: Celestial Arts, 1991, 1995.

Moore, Lorrie. *Anagrams*. New York: Warner Books, 1986.

Murdock, Maureen. *The Heroine's Journey*. Boston: Shambhala, 1990.

Northrup, Christiane. *The Wisdom of Menopause: Creating Physical and Emotional Health and Healing during the Change*. New York: Bantam, 2003.

Pennebaker, James W. *Opening Up: The Healing Power of Expressing Emotions*. New York: The Guilford Press, 1990, rev. 1997.

Pert, Candace. *Your Body Is Your Subconscious Mind*. CD. Boulder:

Sounds True, 2000.

_____. *Molecules of Emotion: The Science behind Mindbody Medicine.* New York: Simon and Schuster, 1999.

Ray, Reginald A. *Meditating with the Body.* Course syllabus and audio. Crestone, Colo.: Dharma Ocean Fndn., 2004.

_____. *Touching Enlightenment: Finding Realization in the Body.* Boulder: Sounds True, 2008.

Reeves, Paula M. *Heart Sense: Unlocking Your Highest Purpose and Deepest Desires.* Boston: Conari Press, 2003.

_____. *Women's Intuition: Unlocking the Wisdom of the Body.* Berkeley: Conari Press, 1999.

Remen, Rachel Naomi. *Kitchen Table Wisdom: Stories That Heal.* New York: Riverhead Books, 1996.

Rich, Adrienne. *Diving into the Wreck: Poems 1971-1972.* New York: W.W. Norton, 1973.

Roberts, Debra. *Prasad for Women.* 5-CD set, No. 5, "Divine Femininism." Weaverville, N.C.: Heron Productions, 2006.

Rome, David. "Searching for the Truth That Is Far below the Search." *Shambhala Sun,* September 2004.

Rumi, Jelaluddin. *The Essential Rumi,* trans. Coleman Barks with John Moyne, A.J. Arberry, and Reynold Nicholson. San Francisco: HarperSanFrancisco, 1995.

Scott, Anne. *Serving Fire: Food for Thought, Body, and Mind.* Berkeley: Celestial Arts, 1994.

_____. *Women, Wisdom and Dreams: The Light of the Feminine Soul.* Freestone, Calif.: Nicasio Press, 2008.

Sher, Gail. *One Continuous Mistake: Four Noble Truths for Writers.* New York: Penguin Compass, 1999.

Trout, Susan S. *Born to Serve: The Evolution of the Soul through Service* with a foreword by His Holiness the Dalai Lama. Alexandria, Vir.: Three Roses Press, 1997.

_____. *The Awakened Leader.* Alexandria, Vir.: Three Roses Press, 2005.

Trungpa, Chogyam and Sakyong Mipham. *Cutting through Spiritual Materialism.* Boston: Shambhala Library, 2002

Tutu, Desmond. *God Has a Dream: A Vision of Hope for Our Time.* New York: Doubleday, 2004.

Whitmont, Edward C. *Return of the Goddess: Femininity, Aggression and the Modern Grail Quest.* London: Routledge & Kegan Paul, 1983.

Williams, Terry Tempest. *Refuge: An Unnatural History of Family and Place.* New York: Vintage Books, 1991.

Woodman, Marion. *Conscious Femininity: Interview with Marion Woodman.* Toronto, Ontario, Can.: Inner City Books, 1993.

_____. *Chaos or Creativity.* Cassette tape recording. Pacific Grove, Calif.: Oral Traditions Archives, 1990.

_____. *The Crown of Age: The Rewards of Conscious Aging.* Cassette tape recording. Boulder: Sounds True, 2002.

_____. *Holding the Tension of the Opposites.* Cassette tape recording. Boulder: Sounds True, 1991.

Woolf, Virginia. *A Room of One's Own.* New York: Harcourt, 2005.

_____. *Women and Writing.* Ed. Michele Barrett. New York: Harvest/HBJ Books, 1979.

Selected Books to Inspire and Support Writing Practice

Andrew, Elizabeth J. *Writing the Sacred Journey: The Art and Practice of Spiritual Memoir.* Boston: Skinner House Books, 2005.

Bayles, David and Ted Orland. *Art and Fear: Observations on the Perils (and Rewards) of Artmaking.* Santa Cruz, Calif.: The Image Continuum, 1993.

Brandeis, Gayle: *Fruitflesh: Seeds of Inspiration for Women Who Write.* New York: HarperSanFrancisco, 2002.

Cameron, Julia. *The Artist's Way.* New York: Tarcher/Putnam, 1992.

_____. *The Right to Write.* New York: Tarcher/Putnam, 1998.

Cappacchione, Lucia. *The Creative Journal: The Art of Finding Yourself.* Athens, Ohio: Swallow Press, 1979.

Delaney, Gayle M. *Living Your Dreams: The Classic Bestseller on Becoming Your Own Dream Expert.* New York: HarperCollins. 1996.

De Salvo, Louise. *Writing as a Way of Healing: How Telling Our Stories Transforms Our Lives.* San Francisco, HarperSan Francisco, 1999.

Dillard, Annie. *Holy the Firm.* New York: HarperPerennial. Rev. Ed., 1988.

_____. *The Writing Life*. New York: Harper and Row, 1989.

Ganim, Barbara and Susan Fox. *Visual Journaling*. Wheaton, Ill.: Quest Books, 1999.

Goldberg, Natalie. *Writing Down the Bones: Freeing the Writer Within*. Boston: Shambhala, 1986.

Keyes, Ralph: *The Courage to Write: How Writers Transcend Fear*. New York: Henry Holt, 1995.

Lamott, Anne. *Bird by Bird: Some Instructions on Writing and Life*. New York: First Anchor Books/Random House, 1994.

Rainer, Tristine. *The New Diary: How to Use a Journal for Self-Guidance and Expanded Creativity*. New York: Jeremy P. Tarcher/Putnam, 1978.

Tharp, Twyla. *The Creative Habit: Learn It and Use It for Life*. New York: Simon & Schuster, 2003.

Thomas, Abigail. *A Three Dog Life*. Orlando, Fla.: Harcourt, 2007.

_____. *Safekeeping: Some True Stories from a Life*. New York: Anchor Books, 2000.

_____. *Thinking about Memoir*. New York: Sterling Publishing Co./ AARP, 2008.

Wooldridge, Susan Goldsmith. *poemcrazy*. New York: Random House, 1996.

Selected Books on Writing Craft

Bernays, Anne and Pamela Painter. *What If? Writing Exercises for Fiction Writers*. New York: HarperPerennial, 1991.

Burke, Carol and Molly Best Tinsley. *The Creative Process*. New York: St. Martin's Press, 1993.

Burroway, Janet. *Imaginative Writing: The Elements of Craft*. New York: Penguin Academics, 2003.

_____. *Writing Fiction: A Guide to Narrative Craft*. New York: HarperCollins, *1996.*

Dufresne, John. *The Lie That Tells a Truth*. New York: W.W. Norton, 2003.

Fowler, H. Ramsey. *The Little, Brown Handbook*. Third Edition. Boston: Little, Brown, 1986.

Hood, Ann. *Creating Character Emotions: Writing Compelling, Fresh Approaches That Express Your Characters' True Feelings*. Cincinnati: Story Press, 1998.

Levasseur, Jennifer and Rabalais, Kevin, Eds. *Novel Voices: 17 Award-Winning Novelists on How to Write, Edit, and Get Published*. Cincinnati: Writers Digest Books, 2003.

McClanahan, Rebecca. *Word Painting: A Guide to Writing More Descriptively*. Cincinnati: Writer's Digest Books, 1999.

Murdock, Maureen. *The Unreliable Truth: On Memoir and Memory*. New York: Seal Press/Avalon, 2003.

Shoup, Barbara and Margaret Love Denman. *Novel Ideas: Contemporary*

Authors Share the Creative Process. Indianapolis: Alpha Books, 2001.

Stein, Sol. *Stein on Writing: A Master Editor of Some of the Most Successful Writers of Our Century Shares His Craft Techniques and Strategies*. New York: St. Martin's Griffin, 1995.

Stern, Jerome. *Making Shapely Fiction*. New York: Doubleday. 1991.

Selected Books on Meditation and Life

Chodron, Pema. *Good Medicine: How to Turn Pain into Compassion with Tonglen Meditation*. Cassette recording. Boulder, Colo: Sounds True, 2001.

_____. *The Places That Scare You: A Guide to Fearlessness in Difficult Times*. Boston: Shambhala, 2002.

_____. *Start Where You Are: A Guide to Compassionate Living*. Boston: Shambhala, 1994.

_____. *When Things Fall Apart: Heart Advice for Difficult Times*. Boston: Shambhala, 2000.

_____. *The Wisdom of No Escape and the Path of Loving-Kindness*. Boston: Shambhala, 1991.

Johnson, Will. *The Posture of Meditation: A Practical Manual for Meditators of All Traditions*. Boston: Shambhala, 1996.

Suzuki, Shunryu. *Zen Mind, Beginner's Mind: Informal Talks on Zen Meditation and Practice*. New York: Weatherhill, 2001.

Selected Books of Poetry

Bowers, Cathy Smith. *The Love That Ended Yesterday in Texas.* Oak Ridge, Tenn.: Iris Press, 1992, 1997.

_____. *Traveling in Time of Danger,* Oak Ridge, Tenn.: Iris Press, 1999.

Collins, Billy. *Ballistics: Poems.* New York: Random House, 2008.

_____. *Sailing Alone around the Room: New and Selected Poems.* New York: Random House, 2002.

_____. *The Trouble with Poetry: And Other Poems.* New York: Random House, 2007.

Cummings, E. E. Edited by George J. Firmage. *Complete Poems 1904-1962.* New York: Norton, 1994.

Flynn, Carolyn Brigit, Ed. *Sisters Singing: Blessings, Prayers, Art, Songs, Poetry and Sacred Stories by Women.* Santa Cruz, Calif.: Wild Girl Publishing, 2009.

Hirshfield, Jane. *The Lives of the Heart: Poems.* New York: Harper-Perennial, 1997.

Hirshfield, Jane, Ed. *Women in Praise of the Sacred: Forty-Three Centuries of Spiritual Poetry by Women.* New York: HarperPerennial, 1994.

Keillor, Garrison, Ed. *Good Poems.* New York: Viking Penguin, 2002.

_____. *Good Poems for Hard Times.* New York: Viking Penguin, 2005.

Oliver, Mary. *New and Selected Poems, Volume One.* Boston: Beacon Press, 1992.

_____. *New and Selected Poems, Volume Two.* Boston: Beacon Press, 2005.

_____. *Red Bird: Poems.* Boston: Beacon Press, 2008.

Sewell, Marilyn, Ed. *Cries of the Spirit.* Boston: Beacon Press, 1991.

Whyte, David. *House of Belonging.* Langley, Wash.: Many Rivers Press, 1996.

_____. *River Flow: New & Selected Poems 1984-2007.* Langley, Wash.: Many Rivers Press, 2007.

About the Author

Based in the Blue Ridge Mountains of North Carolina, Peggy Tabor Millin guides women in the writing process through classes, workshops, and retreats. She is the author of *Mary's Way*, nonfiction articles, short stories, and poetry.

She received her BA in English from University of California, Berkeley. After traveling alone in Europe and the Middle East, she continued her education at Northwestern University, receiving an MA in psychoneurology and communication disorders. She has worked for the Institute of Neurological Sciences, Pacific Medical Center, University of the Pacific, San Francisco; the Department of Vocational Rehabilitation, University of Arizona, Tucson; and the Eastern Band of Cherokee Indians, Cherokee, North Carolina. Other areas of interest include metaphysics, dreams, and Eastern religions.

Ms. Millin welcomes inquiries, comments, or requests for workshops and speaking engagements. For more information, please e-mail her at pmillin@clarityworksonline.com.

About ClarityWorks, Inc.

ClarityWorks, Inc. was founded in 1996 in Asheville, North Carolina. Its mission is to offer programs in the written word that guide women in developing their voice so they can stand in their power and inspire positive change in the world. ClarityWorks' group programs include weekly classes in Asheville and regional and national workshops and retreats. Individualized coaching and mentoring programs are also offered.

In 2009, Ms. Millin established Story Water Press as a division of ClarityWorks with the purpose of publishing her own work, works of ClarityWorks' participants, and the art of Bonnie Temple Cassara.

For more information on ClarityWorks, Inc. or Story Water Press, please contact:

www.clarityworksonline.com
P O Box 9803
Asheville NC 28815
828.298.3863
info@clarityworksonline.com

About Peggy Tabor Millin's Programs and Presentations

With her gentle, welcoming, and encouraging talk, Peggy Millin set the mood for the whole day for all of us. I felt the whole energy of the room shift into a warm, embracing acceptance of everyone present and of our writing (no matter what we might or might not have written), which is so very important to writers, aspiring or already published. Her gentle voice, the kindness of her smile, her careful and attentive listening and response to our questions, our hopes, our fears, our writing created a very special day for me. – Chip Getgood, Words by Women Conference participant

Peggy teaches about writing and courage. I think this is exactly the point of departure for writers. When we accept the scary parts of our writing self, a whole new world opens up, and there's no cheaper way to travel. – Alice Johnson, author of fiction in *O. Henry Festival of Short Stories, The Crucible, Pembroke Magazine, The Guilford Review,* and two anthologies. *I Thought My Father Was God,* ed. Paul Auster and *Alice Redux: Tales of Alice in Wonderland and Lewis Carroll,* ed. Richard Peabody

I have a truth inside me I want to express, a special truth that only I can tell. We all do. That's why we write. And this realization is the great gift that Peggy Millin's classes and retreats have given me—and continue to give me. – Cheryl Dietrich, author of essays in *The Gettysburg Review, Shenandoah, Mudrock Stories and Tales,* and others.

The energy of shared passion and bringing passion to the page. This is what part of the retreat experience has been for me. And then there's Peggy, with her calm and easy presence sharing her wisdom and insights, always supportive, always available when we exude through the experience of putting pen to paper or when we crash in self-doubt with demons wild.... What a difference Centered Writing Practice has made in my life. That alone is THE greatest gift....This is what this sacred circle helped me do—help a beginner begin. The principles were simple: Keep your pen moving, your heart open, your belly soft, kill the "editor," and support the collective. – Betsy Fletcher, poet

..how my writing life has changed since our weekend retreat... I can still feel the peace and beauty of our circle... The writing woman—her heart may break, she may cry out in the pain of her labor, she may even bleed but finally in divine quiet, she will settle back with her sisters in the word and laugh from her gut. – Kathy Godfrey, community college English teacher at work on her first novel

About the Book

Women, Writing and Soul-Making *touched me deeply. It provided the seedling that cracked the sidewalk inside me. It guided me from concrete to fine green grass, from steel rusting as it weathers the storms to nurturing golden wheat floating in soft air and ripening with warm sun. In truth, the book broke me open, and the relief is overwhelming.* – Kelle Olwyler, author with Jerry Fletcher, *Paradoxical Thinking: How to Profit from Your Contradictions*

This book is an invaluable and inspirational resource for anyone wanting to discover the spiritual dimensions of writing, and discovering one's authentic voice. – Angeles Arrien, Ph.D., Cultural Anthropologist, author of *The Four-Fold Way*

I am profoundly touched by Peggy Millin's Women, Writing, and Soul-Making: Creativity and the Sacred Feminine. *As an inspiration for women to reach into the hidden soul and allow it expression, it frames the process of writing in a far larger context than any self-development book. What Peggy is showing us, and leading us toward through her essays and practices, is a deeper journey of service. I felt a great joy of possibility—of women reconnecting with their own feminine soul through writing, to give voice to the Earth. Peggy's book invites us forward as we write, supporting us to risk our desire for security for the wonder of practicing fearless writing as a way of devotion.* – Anne Scott, author of *Women, Wisdom and Dreams: The Light of the Feminine Soul, Serving Fire: Food for Thought, Body and Soul*, and *The Laughing Baby*

Women, Writing, and Soul-Making *has moved me so deeply and is just beautiful. I finished reading it last night and turned back to the first page to read it again. There are so many layers of meaning that I know I will return to it again and again. It is far more than a book on writing—it is a book on being with a capital "B." There is so much wisdom in it.* – Vicki Duncan, therapist and magazine columnist

As a woman writer, I am profoundly grateful to Peggy Millin for treading the path of feminine wisdom, bodily knowing and writing, and illuminating the process for the rest of us. – Demaris S. Wehr, Ph.D. author of *Jung and Feminism: Liberating Archetypes*

LaVergne, TN USA
05 September 2009
157021LV00004B/3/P